Ecclesiastes

INTERPRETATION

A Bible Commentary for Teaching and Preaching

INTERPRETATION

A BIBLE COMMENTARY FOR TEACHING AND PREACHING

James Luther Mays, *Editor*

Patrick D. Miller, *Old Testament Editor*

Paul J. Achtemeier, *New Testament Editor*

WILLIAM P. BROWN

Ecclesiastes

INTERPRETATION

A Bible Commentary
for Teaching and Preaching

John Knox Press
LOUISVILLE

Library of Congress Cataloging-in-Publication Data

Brown, William P., 1958–
    Ecclesiastes / William P. Brown
        p. cm. — (Interpretation, a Bible commentary for teaching and preaching)
    Includes bibliographical references.
    ISBN 0-8042-3146-X (alk. paper)
    1. Bible. O.T. Ecclesiastes—Commentaries. I. Title. II. Series

BS1475.3.B76 2000
223′.807—dc21   99-053620

© copyright William P. Brown 2000
This book is printed on acid-free paper that meets the American National Standards Institute Z39.48 standard. ∞
00 01 02 03 04 05 06 07 08 09—10 9 8 7 6 5 4 3 2 1
Printed in the United States of America
John Knox Press
Louisville, Kentucky

SERIES PREFACE

This series of commentaries offers an interpretation of the books of the Bible. It is designed to meet the need of students, teachers, ministers, and priests for a contemporary expository commentary. These volumes will not replace the historical critical commentary or homiletical aids to preaching. The purpose of this series is rather to provide a third kind of resource, a commentary which presents the integrated result of historical and theological work with the biblical text.

An interpretation in the full sense of the term involves a text, an interpreter, and someone for whom the interpretation is made. Here, the text is what stands written in the Bible in its full identity as literature from the time of "the prophets and apostles," the literature which is read to inform, inspire, and guide the life of faith. The interpreters are scholars who seek to create an interpretation which is both faithful to the text and useful to the church. The series is written for those who teach, preach, and study the Bible in the community of faith.

The comment generally takes the form of expository essays. It is planned and written in the light of the needs and questions which arise in the use of the Bible as Holy Scripture. The insights and results of contemporary scholarly research are used for the sake of the exposition. The commentators write as exegetes and theologians. The task which they undertake is both to deal with what the texts say and to discern their meaning for faith and life. The exposition is the unified work of one interpreter.

The text on which the comment is based is the Revised Standard Version of the Bible and, since its appearance, the New Revised Standard Version. The general availability of these translations makes the printing of a text in the commentary unnecessary. The commentators have also had other current versions in view as they worked and refer to their readings where it is helpful. The text is divided into sections appropriate to the particular book; comment deals with passages as a whole, rather than proceeding word by word, or verse by verse.

Writers have planned their volumes in light of the requirements set by the exposition of the book assigned to them. Biblical books differ in character, content, and arrangement. They also differ in the way they have been and are used in the liturgy, thought, and devotion of the church. The distinctiveness and use of particular books have been taken into account in decisions about the approach, emphasis, and use of space in the commentaries. The goal has been to allow writers to develop the format that provides for the best presentation of their interpretation.

The result, writers and editors hope, is a commentary that both explains and applies, an interpretation that deals with both the meaning and the significance of biblical texts. Each commentary reflects, of course, the writer's own approach and perception of the church and world. It could and should not be otherwise. Every interpretation of any kind is individual in that sense; it is one reading of the text. But all who work at the interpretation of the Scripture in the church need the help and stimulation of a colleague's reading and understanding of the text. If these volumes serve and encourage interpretation in that way, their preparation and publication will realize their purpose.

The Editors

AUTHOR'S PREFACE

It is simply too tempting to introduce yet another commentary on Ecclesiastes without citing the well-known observation of perhaps the book's earliest commentator: "Of making many books there is no end" (Eccl. 12:12). I have come to recognize a certain irony in this universal truth. Given Qoheleth's negative view of human discourse, Ecclesiastes is the one book of the Bible that would seem to discourage, if not sabotage, any attempt at writing a commentary on it (e.g., 1:8–11; 5:2–3, 7 [Heb. vv. 1–2, 6]; 6:11; 12:12). Yet commentaries on what some have called the strangest book in the canon have all but proliferated in the last few years. In my own struggle over the prospect of adding to the growing pool, I have often wondered whether the literary and sapiential enigmas that abound in Ecclesiastes seriously undermine the legitimacy of the commentary enterprise as it is conventionally undertaken.

At the very least, Ecclesiastes exposes the practice of commentary writing as a daunting, if not thoroughly ambivalent, enterprise. A case in point is the work of the book's editors, who attempt to situate the words of Qoheleth within the biblical mainstream, yet in so doing mitigate the provocative nature of his message (12:9–14). Qoheleth's wisdom, frequently iconoclastic and rife with tension, subverts tidy explication and defies coherent summarizing. Any commentator on Ecclesiastes faces a hermeneutical dilemma that is only exacerbated by the numerous contradictions in the text. On the one hand, it is incumbent upon the exegete to be imaginatively empathetic with the "world of the text"; hence, the content and contours of the text should help shape the tone and message of the commentary. On the other hand, given Qoheleth's allegedly all-encompassing perception on the human condition ("In my vain life I have seen everything" [7:15a]), the book also invites critical engagement, even protest, on the part of the interpreter (cf. 7:27; 11:9). Moreover, the veracity of Qoheleth's wisdom, which rests not so much on divine revelation as on the experiences of a "vain life," creates a virtually level playing field between Qoheleth the sage and the modern interpreter who would dare to engage him. The ancient sage invites human discourse while at the same time eviscerating it. Call it Qoheleth's revenge!

In short, there is much in Ecclesiastes that both cripples the traditional commentary enterprise, which seeks coherence in defense of the text's authority, and promotes codified reflection from the reader's perspective. A commentary true to the book's ethos must walk a fine line between explicating the text without necessarily defending it and critically engaging the text without entirely dismissing it. Most appropriate, perhaps, is a dialogical model of commentary reflection that encourages forthright, rather than covert, negotiation between the world of the ancient text and that of the commentator in the shared quest to understand human existence and divine providence, the sage's expressed aims. Indeed, such a model is what drives much of Qoheleth's own discourse as he converses with himself (1:16; 2:1; 7:23) and with traditional forms of wisdom (e.g., 2:14; 4:5–6; 7:7; 8:1). At the very least, recognizing this dimension of the sage's discourse frees up the need to establish a rigid correspondence between the ancient author's worldview and that of the commentator, yet it also guards against the temptation to suppress one in favor of the other. Ecclesiastes, in short, may very well pave the way for a truly postmodern commentary, one that eschews any effort to wrest authoritative coherence from its self-consuming content.

But just such a commentary, in its purest form at least, will have to wait. For now, the way is open for the commentator to acknowledge his or her critical biases in working with the text, while allowing the text to question and probe the commentator in all its strangeness. Hence, a hermeneutics of trust and a hermeneutics of suspicion must remain simultaneously operative, as they were for Qoheleth in his quest to understand his "text," namely, the world of experience.

As a minister of the Word and Sacrament, I initially found myself coming to Ecclesiastes with a negative bias against Qoheleth's rampant skepticism and despairing tone. However, I have come to recognize a wealth of insight from this ancient sage that can actually stimulate fruitful theological reflection, even though logical, including theological, coherence remains an elusive construct for the book. Implicitly recognized by the biblical tradents and early rabbis, there is—to borrow a phrase from Tom Beaudoin—a certain *sensus infidelium* about Ecclesiastes, the "powerful possibility that truth could emerge from those least assumed to be in possession of it" (Beaudoin, p. 34). The irony is that Qoheleth begins his quest for understanding with the glorious hope of possessing all truth, but in the end he grasps only a glimmer. But it is that glimmer that conveys the sage's most profound discovery, ambiguous as it is.

To discern such truth amid the ambiguity of Qoheleth's discourse is the aim of this commentary. In making a contribution to a commentary series that explicitly addresses the church, I am challenged to search expressly for those elements in Qoheleth's discourse that would edify Christian reflection and in particular help pastors, educators, and students to discern Qoheleth's place within the larger witness that is called Scripture. Yet to do so without blunting what is distinctly Qoheleth's is a daunting task. Whether I have successfully preserved the essence of Qoheleth's thought is left for the expert to adjudicate. Whether I have helped the pastor's proclamation or the educator's teaching of the Gospel through a frequently disparaged and misunderstood biblical sage is the greater challenge.

It is appropriate here to extend special thanks to those who have helped to guide this commentary to its completion in a timely manner. I am indebted to James L. Mays and Patrick D. Miller, my editors, for inviting me to write the commentary. Jim's encouragement and guidance have been instrumental from beginning to end in ways he will never know. Thanks also go to the staff of Westminster John Knox Press for their work and patience in preparing the manuscript for publication. Special thanks also go to Naoto Kamano, who graciously reviewed a draft of the commentary while he was conducting his own research on Qoheleth. "Nate" has helped me come to a greater appreciation of the complex rhetoric and ethos of Qoheleth's discourse. In addition, I express appreciation to my students and colleagues of Union Theological Seminary and the Presbyterian School of Christian Education, who have borne the burden of my reflections on Qoheleth, both in and outside the classroom. This commentary is in part a distillation of those conversations.

On more familial territory, I am inestimably grateful to my wife, Gail King Brown, and our children, Ella and Hannah, who taught me a thing or two about the "glory of the ordinary" while I labored over this daunting project. Finally, I dedicate this work to two individuals who are no longer living, much to my loss. My wise grandmother, Mary George Brown, taught me much about the simplicity and practicality of faith. She considered her imminent death as nothing less than a cosmic event. And so it was. This work is also dedicated to Leon McCoy Seaton-Todd. Cut down in his prime by an auto accident, Lee was a gifted and winsome servant of the Word who modeled humility and love for his congregation. He embodied and shared the joy of life in Christ. Though death has taken them both—absurdly so in Lee's case—they remain very much alive in memory while enjoying the fruits of the Resurrection.

CONTENTS

INTERPRETATION

Introduction

Once upon a time in a distant land there lived a king who achieved unsurpassed wisdom. Journeying to the ends of the earth, he overcame insurmountable odds as he devoted himself to searching out the meaning of life. For future generations he recorded his toil and achievements, unmatched by any king before or after him. Yet for all his heroic endeavors, he became painfully aware that no advantage was to be gained for human beings. He was a "man of joy and woe." His name was Gilgamesh, ruler of Uruk, "king of Earth."

In another land and at a much later time, there lived a king who devoted himself to discerning the meaning of life in all matters. He surpassed all who were before him in achievement and wisdom, dedicating himself to the singular pursuit of wisdom. He, too, recorded his arduous struggle in order to counsel future generations of his discoveries. A man of joy and woe, he likewise found that for all his toil "there was nothing to be gained under the sun." His name was Qoheleth, "king over Israel" (see commentary on 1:1).

The book of Ecclesiastes has been deemed the strangest book of the Bible (Scott, p. 191). But despite all that seems perplexing and incongruous about this small work in relation to the larger biblical witness, its anguished message is almost as old as literary history itself. Separated by over two millennia, Gilgamesh and Qoheleth find themselves on essentially the same journey, namely, to find meaning within the finitude of human existence. They are the legendary seekers from antiquity. For women and men today who find themselves on this ancient yet perennial odyssey, seeking both counsel and experience to satisfy their longings for meaningful existence in a seemingly impersonal world, the journey that Gilgamesh and Qoheleth share may be an apt point of departure.

To introduce Ecclesiastes properly, it is helpful to chart something of the book's own journey, from its prehistory within ancient Near Eastern wisdom to its inclusion in the Hebrew Scriptures. (The book's theological place in the Christian witness will be explored in the Epilogue of the commentary.)

1

Qoheleth's Perennial Journey

The journey of Ecclesiastes begins with the so-called *Epic of Gilgamesh*. Many of the values and perspectives shared by the designated spokesperson of Ecclesiastes, "Qoheleth," find their precedent in this dramatic Mesopotamian tale. Written in the cuneiform language of Babylonia (Akkadian), the *Epic of Gilgamesh* is perhaps the greatest literary composition of prebiblical times. Although most of the extant sources of this masterpiece come from the seventh century B.C., they draw from earlier versions that date to the early second millennium, which in turn are dependent upon even more ancient and shorter Sumerian epics. (For a detailed examination, see Tigay, *The Evolution of the Gilgamesh Epic*.) This grand epic concerns itself with the adventures and travails of a certain ruler of Uruk (biblical Erech [Gen. 10:10]), located on the northern bank of the Euphrates in southern Babylonia. Although no contemporary inscriptions of Gilgamesh are yet known, he is believed to have assumed the throne sometime around 2600 B.C. The epic draws from his legendary status as the incomparable king destined for fame.

Because it is always good to include a story in a sermon, it is appropriate to introduce Qoheleth by retelling the dramatic story from which the sage draws much of his reflections. Although scholars have long recognized certain parallels between the epic and the essay, the connections run much deeper and are not limited simply to particular lines or phrases (cf. Jones, pp. 349–79). The occasional citations of the epic given below are drawn primarily from two accessible, though occasionally differing, translations: those of Maureen G. Kovacs and Stephanie Dalley.

The epic begins with an invitation to inspect and marvel at the mighty walls of Uruk, whose imposing contours and craftsmanship are unparalleled. Such construction serves to introduce the epic's protagonist, the man behind the monuments, who is granted the "totality of knowledge" and is described as two-thirds divine and one-third human (Kovacs, p. 3). Unsurpassed in strength, Gilgamesh oppresses the young men and women of Uruk by his overbearing rule and sexual prowess, prompting the town's citizens to petition the gods for intervention. In the heavenly realm, the problem is quickly identified: Gilgamesh lacks a rival; he needs a partner who is both his match and his friend. Enkidu is thus created, a man of the wilderness whose strength and boldness is a worthy match for the godlike Gilgamesh, "who struts his power over the people like a wild bull" (Kovacs, p. 9). Reared in the wild, this primal man lacks, however, the necessary acculturation to enter the fold of civilized life. He also has a habit of setting free animals trapped by

2

hunters. As a remedy, a certain hunter devises a plan to lure Enkidu away from his natural element. To Shamhat, a prostitute, falls the task of socializing this man of the wild. After prolonged love-making, Enkidu finds that he has become alien to his former partners of the wild: "Enkidu was diminished, his running was not as before. But . . . his understanding had broadened" (Kovacs, p. 9). As Shamhat proclaims, "You are beautiful, Enkidu, you are become like a god" (Ibid.). And so Enkidu is initiated into the ways of civilized life; indeed, he must be shown how to eat bread and drink beer, the customs of civilization. Sated, Enkidu "became expansive and sang with joy! He was elated and his face glowed. He splashed his shaggy body with water, and rubbed himself with oil, and turned into a human" (Kovacs, p. 16n. 2 [Old Babylonian Version]).

The stage is now set for the inevitable confrontation with Gilgamesh, who comes to the house of his father-in-law for his wedding. But Enkidu bars the way, preventing the king from meeting his bride. A fight of tectonic proportions ensues, causing walls and doorframes to shake throughout the public square. Eventually, Enkidu wins the fight, and Gilgamesh turns away in defeat and self-disgust (see Kovacs, p. 18). But Enkidu speaks to Gilgamesh with glowing respect for his strength and kingship. They embrace each other. The divine mission is accomplished.

No sooner do they become lifelong friends than Enkidu becomes filled with self-loathing. In his new life, the erstwhile man of the wild has now grown soft. So Gilgamesh proposes a dangerous expedition to kill the mighty Humbaba, the guardian of the Cedar Forest and "terror to human beings" (Kovacs, p. 19). Enkidu reacts with fear, but Gilgamesh responds with proverbial advice: "Who, my Friend, can ascend to the heavens? (Only) the gods can dwell forever with Shamash. As for human beings, their days are numbered, and whatever they keep trying to achieve is but wind! . . . Should I fall, I will have established my fame" (Kovacs, pp.19–21). While human mortality is a given, some form of immortality can be achieved through heroic achievement. The wise counselors of Uruk, however, are less convinced and warn Gilgamesh that such a plan is simply the result of their youthful impetuosity: "You are young, Gilgamesh, your heart carries you off" (Kovacs, p. 21). But realizing that nothing will deter these two youths who would be heroes, the elders deliver a parting word of advice for Gilgamesh: "Gilgamesh, do not put your trust in (just) your vast strength. . . . 'The one who goes on ahead saves the comrade'" (Kovacs, p. 25). Gilgamesh and Enkidu must collaborate if there is any hope of conquering the fearsome Humbaba.

As veritable brothers, they embark on a road "never traveled," equipped for mortal combat against the beast appointed by the high god

3

Enlil to preserve his sacred forest. As they draw close to the forbidden forest, Enkidu has second thoughts and becomes paralyzed with fear. As the elders counseled Gilgamesh, so Gilgamesh counsels Enkidu in the value of teamwork against such seemingly insurmountable odds. Moreover, whether they win or die, they will achieve lasting fame as heroes. Such counsel seems to convince Enkidu to continue the journey. Once they confront the horrible Humbaba, however, it is Gilgamesh's turn to be seized by fear. Enkidu, in turn, must encourage his friend with proverbial advice: "'A three-ply rope *cannot be cut.*' 'The mighty lion— two cubs *can roll him over*'" (Kovacs, p. 37).

To make a long story short, Humbaba is killed by this indomitable team. As Gilgamesh and Enkidu, washed and well dressed, return as victors to Uruk, the city's patron goddess Ishtar proposes marriage to Gilgamesh. Gilgamesh ungraciously declines her offer, noting that all of Ishtar's former lovers had not fared well. This sends the goddess into a fury, prompting her to unleash the fierce Bull of Heaven upon the impertinent king. But Gilgamesh and Enkidu prove old hands at cattle wrestling and are able to kill it. And to add injury to insult, Enkidu shamelessly slaps Ishtar in the face with the bull's shoulder. "Who is the bravest of men . . . the boldest of men?" Gilgamesh rhetorically asks, as the victors stride through the town's main street (Kovacs, p. 56).

Having reached the height of their physical prowess and self-esteem, Enkidu receives a dream in which the holy assembly of the gods convenes a trial and passes judgment against him and Gilgamesh. Enlil demands the death penalty, but the sun god Shamash intercedes on Gilgamesh's behalf. Gilgamesh is spared, but Enkidu is doomed to die. Enkidu is disconsolate. He bitterly complains that a certain doorway he had carefully constructed out of material taken from the majestic Cedar Forest will be owned by someone else: "[T]he king who shall arise after me shall go through you, Gilgamesh shall go through your portals / And change (?) my name, and put on his own name!" In a fit of anger, Enkidu tears out the door and shatters it. The doomed man then expresses regret over having ever come to Uruk and curses the prostitute Shamhat for having acculturated him, and eventually he curses Gilgamesh. In unspeakable grief, Enkidu describes the abode of the dead as the "house of Darkness . . . where those who enter do not come out, along the road of no return . . . where those who dwell do without light, where dirt is their drink, their food is of clay" (Kovacs, p. 65). While Gilgamesh attempts to console his dying friend, ensuring him of a glorious funeral, Enkidu crosses the threshold into death.

Inconsolable, Gilgamesh cannot come to terms with his friend's death. In his own words, "My friend whom I love deeply, who went through every hardship with me . . . the fate of mankind has overtaken

4

him. Six days and seven nights I mourned over him, and would not allow
him to be buried until a maggot fell out of his nose" (Kovacs, p. 85). So
Gilgamesh roams the wilderness, donning lion skin and letting thick hair
grow over his body: Gilgamesh has taken on Enkidu's former nature. But
bitter grief turns quickly into abject dread: "I am going to die!—Am I not
like Enkidu?. . . I fear death, and now roam the wilderness" (Kovacs, pp.
75, 91). In the desperate hope of thwarting the inevitable, Gilgamesh
journeys to locate the one figure who is renowned for having escaped the
clutches of death, the Babylonian Noah, Utanapishtim (elsewhere known
as Atrahasis, "Extra-wise"). The despondent king travels to the ends of
the earth to find this elusive figure and, while on his journey, encounters
a female tavern owner who imparts sage advice:

> Gilgamesh, whither rovest thou?
> The life thou pursuest thou shalt not find.
> When the gods created mankind,
> Death for mankind they set aside,
> Life in their own hands retaining.
> Thou, Gilgamesh, let full be thy belly,
> Make thou merry by day and by night.
> Of each day make thou a feast of rejoicing,
> Day and night dance thou and play!
> Let thy garments be sparkling fresh,
> Thy head be washed; bathe thou in water.
> Pay heed to the little one that holds on to thy hand,
> Let thy spouse delight in thy bosom!
> For this is the task of [mankind]!
>
> (Pritchard, p. 90)

But Gilgamesh will not be assuaged by her commendation of familial contentment and ordinary living. Spurred on by grief and desper-
ation, the undaunted hero is out to seize eternity itself. Venturing forth
where no mortal has gone before, Gilgamesh finally encounters
Utanapishtim, who gives him a sobering assessment of his life by reminding him that death is inevitable. "You have toiled without cease,
and what have you got? Through toil you wear yourself out, you fill your
body with grief, your long lifetime you are bringing near (to a premature
end)!" the immortal sage admonishes Gilgamesh (Kovacs, pp. 92–93).
"Nobody sees Death, Nobody sees the face of Death, Nobody hears the
voice of Death. Savage Death just cuts humankind down. . . . Their faces
look upon the face of the Sun, (but then) suddenly there is nothing. The
sleeping (?) and the dead are just like each other, Death's picture cannot be drawn. . . . The Anunakki, the great gods, . . . appointed death and
life. They did not mark out days for death, But they did so for life" (Dalley, pp. 108–9).

Never satisfied, Gilgamesh demands that Utanapishtim give

5

account of himself and his immortality, to which the sage recounts his story, his "secret of the gods." Utanapishtim was spared the flood only because the god of wisdom (Ea) favored him and offered him the means to escape. "Now then," the sage concludes his account, "who will convene the gods on your behalf, that you may find the life that you are seeking?" Gilgamesh laments, "The Snatcher has taken hold of my flesh, in my bedroom Death dwells, and wherever I set foot there too is Death!" (Kovacs, pp. 104–5). Gilgamesh has no choice except to leave. The heroic king, two-thirds divine, came "exhausted and worn out," not able even to resist sleep, and now must depart empty-handed. But Utanapishtim's wife takes pity on Gilgamesh and suggests to her husband that he provide him with something to take back. So the legendary sage divulges another divine secret by informing the disillusioned hero of a special plant that flourishes in the watery depths and has the power to rejuvenate. In jubilation, Gilgamesh calls this plant by his own name, which means "The Old Man Becomes a Young Man" (Kovacs, p. 106). With renewed hope, Gilgamesh finds the plant and resolves to first try it out on an elder back home. On his return journey, Gilgamesh finds a cool resting place by a pool, and as he refreshes himself a snake silently steals the plant, leaving behind its scaly skin and a despondent warrior.

"For what purpose," cries out Gilgamesh, "have my arms grown weary? For what purpose was the blood inside me so red? I did not gain an advantage for myself, I have given the advantage to the 'lion of the ground,'" that being the snake (Dalley, p. 119). Although Gilgamesh is left empty-handed after all, he does not return a broken man. He comes home resigned and composed, perhaps even able to take himself not so seriously, acknowledging that in his blunder he has rendered a valuable service to the snake (so Jacobsen, p. 208)! The epic ends where it began: with effusive attention given to the walls of Uruk, majestic and enduring, as testimony to this "man of joy and woe" (Dalley, p. 57), ensuring his legacy of triumph and failure. Yet something significant about the protagonist's character has changed. Gilgamesh began as an eminently heroic figure—no less two-thirds divine—and he has completed his journey demythologized, stripped of his divinity, as it were, yet now willing to embrace his mortality and live within the glory of the ordinary.

The purpose of this retelling is not simply to tell a good story from antiquity but to lay the groundwork for understanding the book of Ecclesiastes in its larger ancient Near Eastern context. The sage behind the book, Qoheleth, has woven numerous elements drawn from this epic of a king who would be immortal into his own testimony about a

6

king who would be immortalized in memory. Like Gilgamesh, Qoheleth searches hither and thither for some sense of meaning and purpose before death's inescapable presence. Like the heroic king of Uruk, this sage comes to witness everything "under the sun," human life in both its excess and its frailty, its totality and its "vanity." In his search for some lasting advantage or gain in this life, Qoheleth finds death omnipresent and God inscrutable. Like Gilgamesh, Qoheleth comes back from his journey, his investigation, empty-handed, yet with renewed appreciation of his "vain life."

There is, of course, much distinctive about Ecclesiastes in comparison to the Babylonian epic. The biblical book was written in a time far removed from the Old Babylonian empire. Once the central power in the ancient Near East, Babylon was no more from the author's historical standpoint. Yet the ancient epic remained well known and its themes universal—the dread of death, the futility of human existence, the bond of fellowship, the import of joy and contentment, the inscrutable will of the divine, and the bankruptcy of heroism. In the hands of an Israelite sage, such themes are reinterpreted for a new age, an age of disillusionment.

Ecclesiastes *in situ*

It is likely that the book of Ecclesiastes was produced during the time of cultural malaise that gripped much of the ancient world beginning with the Persian period. It was a time of turbulent socioeconomic change that prompted many to question the wisdom of the past. A number of tomb "biographies"—in some cases autobiographies—from the Late Period in Egyptian history, for example, reflect the spiritual anguish of the times through the mouth of the deceased. They stress, for example, the omnipotence of death, the inscrutability of the gods, and discontinuity in life at the expense of conventional norms (see Burkes, pp. 255–59). The same could also be said about much Hellenistic literature of this time, particularly of the philosophical variety. In short, Qoheleth was a product of his *Zeitgeist*, an age of melancholy and questioning, a culture of death and disillusionment. Such parallels, particularly from Egypt, confirm what is painfully clear about Qoheleth's "autobiography": Ecclesiastes is in a fundamental sense an obituary, indeed the obituary of life itself. As H. Wheeler Robinson sensitively noted, "The book has indeed the smell of the tomb about it" (Robinson, p. 258).

Whether or not one can fit Ecclesiastes confidently into the genre of fictionalized autobiography, as Tremper Longman III does (Longman, pp. 15–20), the prominence of autobiographical material in the book likely reflects something of the book's cultural context. The

7

rise of the specific genre of autobiography—as commonly identified by modern literary scholars with Augustine's *Confessions* (398 A.D.)—has been associated with "the breakup of the traditional community, an increasing sensitivity to change, a shift from deductive to inductive modes of thought, the alteration of the class structure, and increased literacy" (Gunn, p. 7). One can, of course, go too far in extrapolating the cultural context of one age and imposing it on another. But in the case of this genre, Ecclesiastes does not discount a striking level of correspondence between its intensely personal style and a cultural context characterized by profound disillusionment with the past, uncertainty about the future, and a groping for new answers. As Qoheleth reminds the (post) modern reader of today, there is nothing new under the sun.

That Qoheleth's thought and style suggest a relatively late date of composition compared with many other writings of the Old Testament is confirmed linguistically. Persian loan words, Aramaisms, and late developments in Hebrew form and syntax all indicate a fourth or third century B.C. dating for the book. Choon-Leong Seow has recently proposed a more specific time frame within the early fourth (or even late fifth) century based on the use of the verbal root *šlṭ* in fifth-century Aramaic economic documents (Seow, *Ecclesiastes,* pp. 12–21; idem, "Linguistic Evidence," pp. 643–66). However, as Dominic Rudman points out, the economic nuance of this term evidently survives into the Hellenistic period (Rudman, pp. 47–52). For the time being at least, the debate over the specific dating of Ecclesiastes is not fully resolved. The presence of foreign loan words in the text of Ecclesiastes indicates that the Persian period marks the earliest possible dating of Qoheleth's discourse. The lack of any reference to the politically turbulent times when Israel bounced back and forth between the Seleucid and Ptolemaic reigns of the mid-third to late-second centuries *may* make a third-century dating less likely, but this is by no means decisive (so Burkes, p. 39).

What is particularly revealing for understanding the message of Qoheleth is the sociohistorical context of the Persian/early Hellenistic period. Judah had suffered the ravages of defeat and exile by the Babylonians (597–538 B.C.). With the fall of the Babylonian empire under the Persian king Cyrus II in 539, Judah came under Persian hegemony, marked by the release of the exiles by royal edict in 538. Although Judah enjoyed a measure of autonomy (relative at least to what it suffered under earlier empires), it still had to contend with surviving under foreign control. Such was Judah's challenge throughout the remaining centuries of the first millennium B.C. as it passed from Persian to Hellenistic to Roman empires until Jerusalem's destruction in 70 A.D.

Beginning in the Persian period (539–337 B.C.), certain socioeconomic developments occurred that dramatically and indelibly changed the social landscape of Palestine. In contrast to the largely subsistence agrarian economy of preexilic Judah, the economy became increasingly commercialized beginning in the fifth century (Seow, *Ecclesiastes,* p. 23). A standardized monetary currency was introduced for the first time in order to facilitate commerce from Egypt to Persia. In addition, an efficient and aggressive system of taxation was implemented under Persian hegemony. Consequently, a new market-driven economy of global proportions emerged, complete with many entrepreneurial opportunities. Yet such rapid growth did not benefit all people equally. Those who already had extensive capital outlays possessed unprecedented opportunity for cultivating greater assets. Those of lesser means, however, were at a distinct disadvantage. As a result, a shrinking middle class felt overwhelmed with the plethora of economic opportunities and risks. A person could reap profit one day and find himself or herself in the dumps the next day, so volatile was this economy.

Qoheleth reflects the anxiety and hopes that such an emerging economy inspired among the general populace of Judah (e.g., 5:10–12; 7:12; 10:19). Indeed, the sage cuts to the chase in his opening reflections about the human condition by posing the question of economic gain in 1:3: "What do people gain from all the toil at which they toil under the sun?" (see also 3:9; 5:16). Elsewhere, Qoheleth complains of the stranger who receives the earned wealth of another, perhaps reflecting the arbitrariness of the Persian system of royal grants (6:1–2; 2:19–21; see Seow, *Ecclesiastes,* p. 25). Qoheleth's discourse reflects the lack of security and well-being felt among ordinary citizens. As Gilgamesh addressed the issue of immortality through the bankruptcy of heroic achievements, so Qoheleth addresses the issue of lasting gain amid the vicissitudes of an ever-changing social world. In both, the problem of death and tragic happenstance dominates. All that is assured within the realm of experience, Qoheleth points out, is death, the great divester of opportunity. Yet human civilization from remembered time to the current age of virtual reality, like Gilgamesh, has valiantly tried to circumvent this unremitting fact of life.

It is commonly assumed that Qoheleth, as sage, traveled only among the upper echelons of society. But the issue is in fact quite murky. To complicate matters, the sage speaks admiringly of the wise but poor youth and of the sage whose advice was not needed because he was poor (4:13–16; 9:15–16). He laments that bread is not guaranteed to the wise (9:11) and contemptuously looks at the rich, condemning the obsession with wealth as greed (5:10–17). Qoheleth, no doubt, was a man of some means; an illiterate peasant he was not. But

9

one cannot claim that Ecclesiastes is merely a book by the rich for the rich. Its scope is much broader and complex. The same can also be said of the sage's audience, who live under the oppression of unremitting toil, are stricken with anxiety over the prospect of losing their possessions, are frustrated by the loss of justice in the land, and cower in fear before royalty. Such is Qoheleth's world, "vain" as it is.

The meat of the book is, however, not confined to Qoheleth's reflections on economic problems. Its unflinchingly realistic perspectives on the value of life have compelled both ancient and modern interpreters to consider it something of a misfit within the biblical canon. Indeed, the first literary response to Qoheleth's instructions appears within the book itself, namely in its final verses (12:9–14), which serve to summarize and endorse the character of Qoheleth's message, but in so doing they blunt the book's subversive edge in order to bring it into the biblical mainstream. Included in the canon, Ecclesiastes came to be lodged among the poetic books of the Bible, most notably in the so-called wisdom corpus, which also includes Proverbs, Job, and perhaps the Song of Songs.

But it was evidently not easy. A debate ensued about the book's status during the so-called Council of Jamnia by the end of the first century A.D. Apparently there was a division in the house or, more accurately, a conflict between two schools that came to a head during this session of the rabbinic academy: the more conservative House of Shammai, which rejected the book, and the House of Hillel, which approved it. The former claimed that Ecclesiastes was internally contradictory and that some of its views were heretical (e.g., Eccl. 11:9; Num. 15:39). But the book held its own, no doubt owing in part to the book's claim to Solomonic authorship and to its openness to orthodox interpretation (see Eccl. 12:9–14). Much later, by the tenth century A.D., Ecclesiastes came to be associated with one of the great festivals of the Jewish liturgical year, the Feast of Booths (*sukkot*), known in Jewish liturgy as "the season of our rejoicing." Esteemed more for its somber tone and melancholic message than for its affirmation of joy by modern interpreters, the book bears more than an ironic association with this festival. Nevertheless, such a liturgical linkage highlights the frequent commendations of joy found in Qoheleth's discourse. Like Gilgamesh, Qoheleth is "a man of joy and woe." Arguing over whether Ecclesiastes is either optimistic or pessimistic is sort of like trying to determine whether Stravinsky's *The Rite of Spring* is happy or sad. Such profound works cannot be shackled to simple categories.

10

As noted above, a contributing factor to the canonical status of Ecclesiastes in the Hebrew canon was its association with Solomon. As the Psalter became associated with King David, so Proverbs, Ecclesiastes, and the Song of Songs came to be identified with his son (see Prov. 1:1; 10:1a; Eccl. 1:1; Cant. 1:1). In biblical tradition, Solomon is described as the consummate patron of wisdom (1 Kings 3—4), having composed 3000 proverbs and 1005 songs (4:32). According to later rabbinic tradition, the Song of Songs was written by Solomon in his youth, Proverbs in his prime, and Ecclesiastes in his old age. Although historically suspect, such a claim suggests a way of understanding much of the wisdom corpus as a veritable compendium of experience and learning that spans all the stages of life, from youth to wise sage. As will be shown in the commentary, the character of Solomon serves as both Qoheleth's guise and foil. As soon as the sage dons the Solomonic mantle (1:12—2:12), he disposes it in order to convey his harsh judgments about the futility of "gainful" living. Here, too, early Jewish tradition, as reflected in the Targum, noted this significant shift by claiming that Solomon was driven from his throne and destined by God to roam the world, weeping and lamenting (see Levine, p. 28). In any case, Qoheleth is a composite character who embodies the yearnings of an ambitious king and the harsh judgments of a critical sage, perspectives also found among the contrasting figures of Gilgamesh, Šiduri, and Utanapishtim in the Babylonian epic. "You have toiled without cease, and what have you got?" Utanapishtim asks the weary king Gilgamesh. It is the same question Qoheleth asks himself.

Qoheleth's struggle is mythic in the sense that it resonates with each generation, ancient or contemporary. In his ruminations, the sage subtly moves from king to ordinary mortal, following a venerable literary scheme that is found even among modern-day sports stories. It is no accident that the most intriguing stories are not about the athlete at the height of power, when he or she is for a fleeting moment considered immortal, but about how the once glorious athlete deals with matters later in life, including old age. Therein lies the wisdom.

In his journey from the pinnacle of power to the valley of deep darkness, Qoheleth has "seen everything" in his quest to "search out and to seek wisdom and the sum of things" (Eccl. 7:15, 23–25). In addition to similarity in vocabulary and style, Qoheleth's stated aim places his codified reflections squarely within the larger stream of the Bible's sapiential tradition, which itself is somewhat unique among the more familiar traditions of Scripture. Indeed, one could label the wisdom corpus as the Bible's "alternative" tradition. Much has been said about how the wisdom corpus is both different from and contiguous with Yahwistic faith and piety. Briefly put, most conspicuous about the wisdom literature is its "ahistorical" character. Strikingly absent among Proverbs, Job, and Ecclesiastes are the great themes of biblical history,

11

such as the exodus, covenant, and conquest of the land. God's role as deliverer and lawgiver, in turn, is scarcely mentioned in the wisdom traditions. Rather, emphasis is placed upon creation and humanity's place in it. Except in a few places (e.g., Eccl. 5:1), the wisdom traditions do not address issues related to worship so much as they reflect upon life within the household and larger community outside the priestly sphere. Eschewing the grand claims of revelation, biblical wisdom, in short, focuses on the religious and moral dimensions of day-to-day existence, in which ordinary experiences take on an almost incarnational character. The sapiential tradition is the Bible's "theology from below," the stuff of wisdom gained from living "under heaven."

Broadly speaking, the wisdom books treat "wisdom" (*hokmâ* in Hebrew, *sophia* in Greek) as the art of navigating the complexities of life and discerning God's ways in the immediacy of life. They share certain literary conventions, from short aphoristic sayings to lengthy instructions, and common sapiential rhetoric, including the language of intellectual discernment, moral agency, and piety. Indeed, there is even evidence of cross-referencing (e.g., Prov. 26:27 and Eccl. 10:8; Prov. 30:4; Job 38:1–7). One topic that all three canonical books share is the "fear of the Lord" as the foundation to wisdom (Prov. 1:7, 29; Job 28:28; Eccl. 12:13). The wisdom books, in short, provide instruction that is both theologically charged and morally pragmatic; in short, they convey a prudential form of theological ethics.

Yet within this heterogeneous mix, Ecclesiastes stands out. The spokesman of the book, Qoheleth, is not averse to deferring to, even citing from, traditional wisdom, but he does so to reexamine conventional norms and values dialogically. As many have pointed out, the book is rife with contradictions, but the question of whether such contradictions are ever resolved or are left to stand in raw tension is an open question among modern interpreters. Qoheleth's contradictions, at the very least, seem to serve the didactic purpose of subverting facile interpretations of his discourse and heightening the larger ambiguity that engulfs the book. Finding a uniform, determinate meaning in Ecclesiastes is as elusive as securing enduring gain was for the sage behind the book.

Nevertheless certain themes do stand out, particularly the fragility of human existence, the inability of human beings to secure themselves, the inscrutable will of God, and the call to *carpe diem*, to "seize the day" before the sun sets, as it were. These persistent themes render, in my opinion, a coherent theological and ethical orientation, but one unlike anything that is encountered elsewhere in biblical wisdom, much less throughout the Old Testament. Despite its strange fit in the canon, Ecclesiastes must be taken seriously. Qoheleth's credentials are indisputable. Steeped in tradition and endowed with supple intellect, Qoheleth proves himself to be a master of sapiential rhetoric and a keen observer of what goes on "under the sun," that is, of all life and activity under God's inscrutable sovereignty.

Perhaps an appropriate heuristic analogy for describing the relationship between Qoheleth and the more conventional wisdom of the sages can be found in the discipline of music criticism. Most traditional accounts of the development of European music divide the history into distinct periods, although the chronological demarcations can be quite blurry: Renaissance, Baroque, Classical, Romantic, and Modern. Though the historical periods differ considerably in style, form, and—particularly in the modern period—tonality, such a comprehensive view suggests a degree of continuity, a continuum or spectrum, in which one period builds upon its predecessor, while also representing a paradigm shift of sorts. Particularly intriguing is the following analogy: as modern music, complete with harmonic desecration (as in the works of Stravinsky and Schönberg), is to earlier forms, so is Qoheleth's sapiential instruction compared with more "classical" forms of wisdom. Or, to put it crassly, it is awfully difficult to hum Qoheleth's tune.

One clear aim of Qoheleth's agenda, for example, is to whittle down the glorified promises made about wisdom in conventional wisdom (e.g., Prov. 3:13–18; 8:1–21; 11:18–19; 12:28; 13:14). In that sense, Qoheleth could be compared to the so-called minimalist movement in modern music. And yet, not unlike numerous contemporary musical compositions, there is also a "neoclassical" streak in Qoheleth's thought that allows it to be read in more traditional ways. In short, Qoheleth is an eclectic who is more than willing to adopt conventional form and content as he strives to tear down and rebuild the ethos of wisdom. Qoheleth's peculiar pedagogical style, moreover, is rooted in his fluid oscillations between the conventional and the subversive, the classical and the radical, like a pendulum swinging back and forth between contradictions. Some have identified numerous examples of the so-called "yes-but expression," which reflects Qoheleth's inner disputational style (Hertzberg, pp. 29–31). Whether such precision can be determined in such subtle and complex rhetoric, the ancient sage clearly acknowledges both a time to appropriate the traditions of the past and a time to challenge them (cf. Eccl. 3:1–8).

The crisis that Qoheleth represents vis-à-vis conventional wisdom is not so much formal as existential. At root for the sage is the incapacity of the human being to save himself or herself from the hegemony of chance and the indiscriminate onslaught of death. As enduring gain

13

eludes the grasp of every human being, so wisdom cannot guarantee security, much less prosperity, for the practitioner of wisdom. Wisdom, too, is "far off, and deep, very deep; who can find it out?" (Eccl. 7:24). On the one hand, wisdom—like the plant of rejuvenation that slips through Gilgamesh's fingers—is the proverbial lost coin that can never be found. On the other hand, it constitutes the very method behind the all-consuming search for wisdom. Wisdom is Qoheleth's one and only tool for investigating "all that is done under heaven" (Eccl. 1:13). Wisdom enables the sage to formulate the sapiential observations of his predecessors, as well as his own, and to deconstruct them.

The radical nature of many of Qoheleth's observations lies in his turning wisdom against itself. Saul Bellow humorously puts it, "Socrates said, 'The unexamined life is not worth living.' My revision is 'But the examined life makes you wish you were dead'" (Quoted from Gussow, *New York Times,* May 26, 1997). But wisdom does not entirely deconstruct itself any more than Qoheleth advocates suicide for his readers. "A living dog is better than a dead lion" (Eccl. 9:4b). The outcome of the examined life and world is a heightened awareness of life's "vanity" (*hebel*): its futility and fragility, its absurdity and obscurity are all rooted in the inscrutably sovereign will of God.

But that is not all. Inseparably wedded to such awareness is a newly acquired freedom to savor those fleeting moments of enjoyment that allow one to catch flashes of grace amid the absurdity. Such glimpses had been, Qoheleth contends, overlooked by more imperious theological perspectives that attempt to penetrate the very mind of God. Qoheleth's search is all about finding God not in some discernible scheme of history or on some spiritual level suspended above the fray of human existence, but in the details of the daily grind of living. Qoheleth offers modern readers the dread and delight of the everyday, the glory of the ordinary. As Gilgamesh, ruler of Uruk, adumbrates the self-questioning king of Jerusalem, so the biblical sage anticipates Søren Kierkegaard's "knight of faith," who by giving up all claim of possessing anything in life surrenders all to God, "delights in everything he sees," and becomes "a new creation by virtue of the absurd" (Kierkegaard, pp. 50–51). Like Gilgamesh before him, Qoheleth moves in the direction of infinite resignation and infinite faith.

In part by dint of a divided vote in a little-known rabbinic academy at the turn of the first century A.D., Qoheleth's work has left an ambivalent yet indelible imprint upon the rich theology of the scriptural witness. Qoheleth is no agnostic except perhaps when it comes to the precise fate of the soul after death (Eccl. 3:21; but cf. 12:7). Yet his reflections can burst the bubbles of pretension that frequently float to the

14

surface of theological discourse and doctrine. His ruminations embody a theology from below, derived not from the perspective of the socially disadvantaged but from the standpoint of the theologically disillusioned. Qoheleth clears away much theological speculation by stressing time and again the impenetrable and sovereign will of God, to which the absurdities of life point. In this way, Qoheleth, like Paul, is a "steward of God's mysteries" (1 Cor. 4:1). For the ancient sage, the world is in the end not so much a theater of the absurd as the arena of God's mystery. In it, no one can make straight what God has made crooked (Eccl. 7:13). The ancient sage reminds Christians that for all its assurance and promise, great is the mystery of faith.

Literary Structure and Integrity

Not surprisingly, a coherent and tidy literary structure is distinctly lacking in Ecclesiastes. Attempts by scholars at delineating a clear structure through numerical analyses, polar structures, redactional levels, or concentric rings have proved largely unsuccessful. Seeking structure in Qoheleth's turbid discourse is, frankly, an exercise in frustration. Indeed, for a book that capitalizes on uncertainty and stresses the incapacity to understand much of anything, that may not come as a surprise. Nevertheless, Qoheleth's codified reflections do not give the impression of having been haphazardly slapped together either. There is some semblance of development and repetition that intimates something akin to the intensely personal yet deliberately didactic reflections of an anguished sage.

For example, Qoheleth's own discourse is framed by 1:2–11 and 12:1–8. The former opens with the sage's thesis statement regarding the pervasiveness of "vanity," and the latter concludes almost verbatim (1:2; 12:8). The former offers a comprehensive picture of cosmic weariness and repetition that is also reflected in the course of human affairs, a cosmology without creation. The climax of the sage's reflections concludes with a no less encompassing picture of death's encroachment upon the living, extinguishing even the celestial lights (12:2), a creation without continuance. The heart of Qoheleth's message is, thus, bracketed by cosmos and extinction, by weariness and death.

Perhaps one could go a bit further. What follows the sage's cosmology in 1:2–11 are the confessions of a wise king who is dismayed at the inefficacy of his grand accomplishments yet who savors, in the end, the simple delights of eating, drinking, and the benefits of meaningful work (1:12—2:26). By the time one reaches the book's conclusion, the sage has moved from self-reflective language ("I said to myself . . ." [1:16; 2:1, 15; cf. 3:17–18]) to directive language that addresses a young

15

man ("Rejoice, young man . . ." [11:9]). Eric Christianson has noted a significant change in the course of the book from first-person to second-person discourse (Christianson, pp. 244–45). Relatedly, one finds a greater concentration of proverbial sayings in the latter half of the book (e.g., 7:1–13; 9:17–19; 10:1–4, 8–20; 11:1–4). Such an observation suggests at least some measure of pedagogical movement.

Moreover, the move from cosmology to the individual at the beginning of the book and the shift from the individual to the cosmic dimensions of death near the end reveal an inseparable bond between cosmos and corpus. But as one moves further into the body of the book, any hints of a clear structure prove more elusive. The intervening material comprises more of a hodgepodge of reflective and prescriptive material. In short, only the most general of outlines can be proposed, one that is more topically than formally governed (see Crenshaw, pp. 34–49; Seow, *Ecclesiastes,* pp. 43–47).

16

Although not prominently reflected in this topical outline, the physical center of the book is found in 6:10, as noted by the Masoretes.

The thematic center is not far off the mark, which I would identify as 6:10—7:4. In these few verses, the book's prominent themes of death and discourse, vanity and gain, joy and sorrow are all effectively summarized. Such themes are repeated throughout the book almost in refrain-like fashion: the problem of gain or advantage (1:3; 2:11, 22; 3:9; 4:9 ["good reward"]; 5:11 [Heb. v. 10], 16; 6:8), the affirmation of joy (2:24–26; 3:12–13, 22; 5:18–20 [Heb. vv. 17–19]; 7:14; 8:15; 9:7–10; 11:7–10), the indiscriminate nature of death (e.g., 2:14b–16; 3:19–21; 4:2–3; 5:15–16 [Heb. vv. 14–15]; 6:3–5; 7:2, 17; 9:1–6, 10; 12:1–7), and the reference to "vanity" (*hebel*), the book's leitmotif, which not only occurs thirty-seven times throughout the book but also brackets Qoheleth's discourse (1:2; 12:8).

As I read Ecclesiastes, I am struck by the book's intensely personal style, subtle argumentation, and prescriptive power, despite what appears to be a rambling and circuitous manner of presentation. Thus, I am hard-pressed to fit this book within any uniform genre, whether autobiography or diatribe. It is neither straight narrative nor systematic treatise. The work is a messy mixture of autobiographical references, theological reflections, philosophical musings, and proverbial instructions. Ecclesiastes is sui generis in the literary landscape. If pressed to give some classification, I would propose what may seem like an oxymoron: an "autobiographical treatise," a work that combines sophisticated reflection and autobiographical style, a compendium of personal ruminations and instructions. Yet such a thing as Ecclesiastes may not be all that rare, at least not in modern literature. Filled with personal experiences and lessons, the book comes across as the distillation of an investigative journal, the notebook of a resigned cynic.

Understanding Ecclesiastes

Of all the books of the Bible, Ecclesiastes is perhaps the least straightforward (although Job may come a close second). The book's elusive style must be acknowledged at the outset before navigating the murky waters of Qoheleth's discourse. One rule of thumb that applies to understanding any biblical passage is to let the whole interpret the part. This is particularly apropos to Ecclesiastes, although such a strategy does not resolve every feature of the book, rife as it is with tension. On the one hand, for example, the ancient sage laments that "the dead (are) . . . more fortunate than the living" (4:2) and that the "stillborn child is better off than" the patriarch who begets a hundred children but does not receive a burial (6:3). On the other hand, Qoheleth affirms that "a living dog is better (off) than a dead lion" (9:4). So which is it: does the sage favor life or death? One contextual clue for coming to

17

terms with contradictions is offered at the outset of the book: using experience as his guide, Qoheleth as king embarks on a *quest* for meaning (1:12–13). The close of the book offers something of a conclusion (11:7—12:7). The reflections in between are, thus, part of the journey of the sage, whose observations remain provisional and are continually transformed. Indeed, it should be no surprise to find the sage deliberately contradicting himself, even *within* discrete passages. While acknowledging significant distinctions between wisdom and folly, for example, Qoheleth finds such differences of no ultimate value vis-à-vis the common fate that befalls the wise and the foolish, namely, death, the great equalizer (2:12–17). Such distinctions for the sage are at best relative and at worst irrelevant.

As both a method and an object of investigation, wisdom for the sage is ever on the move, taking account of the polarities and obscurities of human existence. Rooted in experience, wisdom for the sage weighs and assesses the vagaries of human existence as he attempts to make sense of his world "under the sun." Consequently, those observations found in the second half of the book may hold greater significance than those lodged in the first. Indeed, Qoheleth's instructions and sayings are cast in a (slightly) more positive light in the latter half of the book, culminating with the sage's instructions in 11:1—12:8. Such movement might suggest a pedagogy that begins with certain negative lines of inquiry, a *via negativa,* as it were, but gradually gives way to more positive, directive instruction. In any case, the arrangement of Qoheleth's ruminations is designed more to provoke reflection—indeed dialogue—among readers, rather than to reach premature, self-assured conclusions. Experience is a harsh yet ultimately inconclusive assayer of doctrine, Qoheleth seems to suggest.

As one epilogist aptly states, Qoheleth's sayings are like "goads" or prods that keep the process of learning unsettled and ongoing. The search for wisdom is a lifelong journey, fraught with bitter disappointments and unexpected delights, profound discovery matched by equally profound disillusionment. In essence, Ecclesiastes is a book about seeking, one that moves between cynicism and acceptance, worldliness and spirituality, anxiety and serenity. In the end, the ancient sage seems to say, "Brace yourself for the inevitable, but while there is still time follow the deepest inclinations of your heart and revel in the glory of the ordinary. But be careful what you seek," for, as Qoheleth's most preeminent successor aptly warned, "[W]here your treasure is, there your heart will be also" (Matt. 6:21).

Ecclesiastes 1:1

Superscription

The opening verse attributes the wide assortment of poetry, proverbs, and autobiographical material that make up much of Ecclesiastes to an enigmatic figure whose character is as complex as his writing is frequently abstruse. Whether as actual author or fictionalized persona, the "Teacher" is credited as the source of most of the material in Ecclesiastes (see 7:27; cf. 12:9–14). Whoever he is or was, the alleged author of the instructional and (auto)biographical material is the book's spokesperson. He bears the title *qōhelet* ("Teacher"), whose verbal root means "to assemble." This would suggest one of two roles for the person behind the title: to convene an assembly (Deut. 4:10; 1 Kings 8:22)—assumed in the Latin transliteration of the Greek *ekklēsiastēs* ("member of the assembly" or "citizen")—or to collect wisdom sayings in codified form (cf. Eccl. 12:11). The latter sense corresponds well to the statement in 7:27, in which Qoheleth's task is described as "adding one thing to another to find the sum." Like an auditor taking an inventory, the "Teacher" sees himself as an investigator who collects and codifies a wealth of observations, both his own and those mediated by tradition. His mission is to find the sum of things, to arrive at a unified account of all that occurs "under the sun."

Whether as a convener of assemblies or an assembler of sayings, "Qoheleth" is the author's nom de guerre, and Solomon is his alter ego. Together, the title and the person are integrally related to Qoheleth's self-characterization as the consummate royal sage (1:12—2:12). But this kingly guise later becomes his foil. As royal sage, Qoheleth has the indisputable credentials to conduct an investigation of the world; he is the unsurpassed student of wisdom and thus the teacher of teachers. And yet, as he will soon discover, such a glorified persona proves to be only a façade on wisdom's level playing field.

That Qoheleth is introduced as king, Solomon in particular, is understandable (see Introduction). According to 1 Kings, Solomon was known for his intellectual acuity and moral discernment, at least during the outset of his reign. His prayer for wisdom at Gibeon (1 Kings 3:1–15), his inventive solution to the contested infant (vv. 16–28), his prodigious literary output, and his encyclopedic knowledge of nature (4:32–34) all attest Solomon's legendary status as the archetypal royal sage of biblical lore. This son of David became the glorious exemplar for all kings in matters of sagacity. Yet only in the first two chapters, beginning with 1:12, does Qoheleth actually develop his Solomonic connection. Like the godlike Gilgamesh, who comes to embrace his mortality, Qoheleth later seems to shed his royal garments, stripping himself, as it were, of the trappings of royalty. His royal identity is only simulated, reflecting a crisis of identity. But whether as king or commoner, victor or failure, Qoheleth offers the results of his investigation—his penetrating observations and advice—to posterity. Qoheleth's royal persona, in short, serves only as his point of departure; it establishes his credentials for the investigative task at hand. Beyond that, Qoheleth's royal identity is largely irrelevant. Indeed, it becomes his straw man.

Christian tradition has long recognized that there may be more to Qoheleth's role than simply that of penetrating cynic. Ever since Martin Luther's translation of the Bible in 1534, the Hebrew title *qōhelet* has typically been translated "the Preacher" (see KJV, RSV). Although the modern reader may be hard pressed to find anything particularly homiletical or uplifting about Qoheleth's words, Luther, drawing from earlier tradition, evidently saw something about the sage's discourse that bore sermonic potential. For Luther, the act of preaching entailed "throw[ing] oneself in the way of Satan's many teeth" (Campbell, p. 384), not a terribly comforting image for anyone who mounts the pulpit on a Sunday morning! But perhaps Qoheleth would agree. There is indeed something confrontational, even self-endangering, about preaching and teaching, and it begins by reckoning with the pathos of our God-given lives.

Proclaiming the Word, Qoheleth reminds us, is about courageously confronting the bewilderingly complex and convoluted world in which people live and move and have their being in God. A sermon, consequently, is not worthy of a hearing unless it reckons with the torturous contingencies of human existence, the turmoil of life, as well as the joy and peace given in Christ. Unless preaching—or more broadly theological education—touches people at these common levels of experience, taking account of both the void and the vitality of life before God, the proclaimed message is simply dead on arrival. Speaking only from the top down, from a pedestal rather than from a pulpit, yields only patronizing pronouncements delicately suspended above the fray of the living, unreachable and irrelevant. The preacher must also be a keen observer of life from the bottom up, as well as a discerning interpreter of the Word given from on high. Qoheleth would remind us that as the Word became flesh, flesh is also made word, a living testimony to divine providence and human creatureliness. Qoheleth's own life—his story and observations—is just such a testimony. His "sermon" is not from the mount but from the depths.

Opening one's eyes to both the painful wrenchings and surprising gifts that comprise the mystery of life is what Ecclesiastes is all about. Qoheleth is no ivory-tower recluse, "collecting" his thoughts in the privacy of his study. Rather, the sage courageously ventures forth to investigate what is *truly* real in all its messiness and mystery. By entering fully into the fray of human existence, the ancient sage is able to "tell it like it is." Qoheleth's odyssey is not a happy journey, but it is an enlightening one. He reminds those who are called to proclaim the Gospel that preaching requires interpreting *both* the Word and the world. Only by confronting life in all its vicissitudes and death in its totalizing scope can one experience the fullness of the mystery of God. Tempting as it is for contemporary preachers, Qoheleth does not evade the void amid the vibrancy of life; indeed, he enters it fully and experiences a greater appreciation of what life holds "on this side." Contrary to what is commonly preached, life is not simply a journey of edifying experiences, a pilgrimage of glee. It is also about confronting inevitable despair, disillusionment, and, yes, death face to face, the *via negativa*. Ecclesiastes, in short, covers the gamut of life down under, that is, "under the sun" and under God. His is a theology from below, not for liberation's sake but for navigating the turbulent waters of the living of these days in reverence to God. Qoheleth is a teacher for preachers who has lived to tell about it all . . . barely.

Ecclesiastes 1:2–11
A Vanity of Cosmic Proportion

As the superscription serves to introduce the book and its central persona or author, so the following section serves as the book's preface to illustrate in vividly cosmic terms Qoheleth's global thesis: "All is *hebel*" (v. 2).

The Verdict of "Vanity" (1:2)

The thematic word *hebel*, the book's leitmotif, is repeated no less than thirty-seven times in Ecclesiastes. It makes its first appearance in

1:2 and its final appearance in almost identical phraseology in 12:8, thereby establishing a literary framework for all of Qoheleth's deliberations. The term *hebel*—identical to the name of Cain's ill-fated brother, Abel, in Genesis 4—*denotes* a vivid image, namely, vapor or breath, while *connoting* something empty and worthless (Isa. 57:13) or useless (30:7; 49:4). Following the KJV, the NRSV retains the translation "vanity," which conveys futility or something done "in vain," but not necessarily out of self-conceit, as associated with the modern usage of the term. Indeed, the English term "vanity" can also signify "emptiness" or "void." For Qoheleth, vapor or "vanity" is a versatile image that suggests certain distinctive nuances according to the particular context in which the term is found. Hence, numerous suggestions have been made concerning the translation of *hebel*, from "ephemerality" and "emptiness," even "meaninglessness," to "absurdity" and "shit" (so Crüsemann, p. 57). Indeed, the NJPSV (Tanakh) translates *hebel* contextually eight different ways (see Fox, "The Meaning of *Hebel* for Qohelet," p. 413).

There is, to be sure, an amorphous quality to the meaning of *hebel* as Qoheleth employs it. Although difficult to translate consistently, the term does serve the general function in Qoheleth's discourse of setting in starkest relief the inefficacy of certain aspects of life that must bear the weight of deeply seated human longings and expectations. "Vanity" is like a mirage, or more pointedly, a fata morgana in which human efforts, hopes, and plans "evaporate" before life's vicissitudes and are replaced by want and misery. "Vanity" is systemic, Qoheleth contends in this opening statement; it is part and parcel of the very structure of life. "Vanity" strips life of all great promises, and any appearances to the contrary are precisely that, mere appearances. As the ultimate source of frustration, "vanity" is unavoidable; it is the brick wall that blocks the headlong rush toward achieving self-gain and glory or, in fact, accomplishing anything. As brother Abel gained God's approval yet gave up his life as the victim of fraternal discontent, so any gain in life, however tangible and secure, can easily "take wings to itself, flying like an eagle toward heaven" (Prov. 23:5).

Qoheleth's verdict of vanity acknowledges that no matter how hard they try, human beings cannot secure themselves or fill the void any more than they can drink water from a mirage. We are not the masters of our destinies, the sage claims, for the wall of human limitation can never be breached. And there is no way around it, for the void of "vanity," as the sage will demonstrate, engulfs both the universal and the individual, both cosmos and corpus. Whatever *hebel* means precisely, the world is full of it!

Cosmos without Creation (1:3–7)

If "vanity" marks the conclusion to Qoheleth's quest, the question that prompts his search is found in the following verse. The query in verse 3, in fact, serves double duty by also introducing the sage's understanding of the cosmos in verses 4–7. The question of gain from toiling "under the sun," that is, within the realm of the living, turns out to be a vexing one for the sage because it cuts to the heart of human activity and identity. Whether for weal or for woe, people do and must work: "In all toil there is profit, but mere talk leads only to poverty" (Prov. 14:23). Labor, in contrast to "mere talk," embodies the exertion necessary for gainful living (cf. 2 Thess. 3:6–13). The question of work also broaches the issue of the world's very nature and purpose.

The cosmos, Qoheleth observes, is typified by toilsome activity. Existence requires exertion. Generations come and go, the sun rises and sets only to return back to where it started, the wind whirls incessantly in its circuitous courses, and streams flow continually without ever filling the sea (Eccl. 1:4–7). The whole world is a scene of incessant movement and activity. But is it purposeful? Qoheleth asks. For all the constant motion that characterizes the cosmos, one would think that something is being accomplished. But no. Even as the millennia come and go, any semblance of progress is only a mirage. Activity abounds; everything is in perpetual motion, like a hamster in a wheel, but no destination is reached. This display of endless cosmic exertion is all for naught. There is nothing dynamic or progressive about cosmic movement, for despite it all the world "remains forever," firmly immutable (v. 4). Yet this provides no consolation for the ancient sage (cf. Isa. 51:6). The perdurability of creation amounts to nothing; it simply reflects the static nature of a creation forever locked in the same wearying courses. Ever in motion, the universe is uniformly indifferent to human living, from birth to death.

What the sage and the psalmist say about the sun illustrates how far apart they are in understanding creation:

> In the heavens [God] has set a tent for the sun,
> > which comes out like a bridegroom from his wedding canopy,
> > and like a strong man runs its course with joy.
> Its rising is from the end of the heavens,
> > and its circuit to the end of them;
> > and nothing is hid from its heat.
> > > (Ps. 19:4b–5 [Heb. vv. 5b–6])

> The sun rises and the sun goes down,
> > and hurries [literally "pants"] to the place where it rises.
> > > (Eccl. 1:5)

23

Qoheleth and the psalmist vividly describe the perceived concentric movement of the sun but in remarkably different ways. From the psalmist's standpoint, the sun bursts forth in its rising with potent force, full of vigor in its procession across the domed sky; in Qoheleth's eyes, the sun gasps for breath from its enervating circuits. For the psalmist, explosive virility and penetrating heat characterize the sun's circuit; the wedding canopy, the scene of consummation and blissful rest (cf. Joel 2:16), marks the sun's departure point as it joyously arcs the sky. For the sage, the sun has aged and grown weak.

As the sun rushes back to its departure point, so all the elements of creation hurry around to no avail. This is a cosmos devoid of *telos* and full of toil, a world without direction and seemingly deprived of its own genesis. Creation elsewhere in the Bible consistently weds genesis and purpose, ontology and teleology, as determined by the divine will. But there is nothing, properly speaking, *creative* about Qoheleth's cosmos; indeed, God does not even appear to be involved. Whereas the venerable creation traditions of Genesis 1—3, Psalm 104, Isaiah, and Job 38—41, among others, boldly claim the world as eminently *created*, wrought by a loving and powerful God, Qoheleth's cosmology, for all intents and purposes, excludes creation. As there is no beginning, there seems also to be no end or, more pointedly, no *sabbath* or ordained rest.

The world according to Qoheleth is an empty cosmos running perpetually like clockwork in its wearying courses. There is no poetry of provision in Qoheleth's cosmological accounting as in the great hymn of creation in Psalm 104. The constant rhythms of day and night are not praised for their salutary roles in sustaining and ordering life (cf. Ps. 104:19–23); they are rather disparaged for their incessant repetitions. According to the psalmist, the gushing streams provide for life, including the "birds of the air" (vv. 10–12). For Qoheleth, they flow for nothing. Qoheleth's world reflects neither God's transcendent glory nor God's immanent presence. Whereas Psalm 104 vividly describes a *creatio continuata*, creation sustained and directed in all of its manifold forms, Qoheleth dolefully describes perpetual uniformity, a monotony of the spheres.

Qoheleth's world is stripped of potency and potential for a reason. Further comparison with other creation traditions of the Bible sheds light on Qoheleth's agenda. Many creation traditions lift up a central image or context that sets the stage for moral living, in short, an *ethos* (literally "habitation" from the Greek). Genesis 1:1—2:3, for example, is structured around carefully delineated domains of habitation (sky, land, and water), particularly between the holy and the good, as also reflected in the architecture of the priestly tabernacle or sanctuary in its

24

larger cultural environment. The creation account in Gen. 2:4b—3:24 is set in a lush garden in which harmony between human nature and vocation, between male and female, and between nature and culture reigns. Another evocative creation account is given in Prov. 8:22–31, in which the cosmos serves as the secure home for child wisdom to grow and delight in. Finally, Job 38—42 profiles creation from the vantage point of the untamed wilderness, in which wild animals live and flourish under God's providential care. The sanctuary, the household, the garden, and the wilderness: each one lies behind a particular creation tradition in the Old Testament. (For a full discussion, see Brown, *The Ethos of the Cosmos*.)

What, then, can be said of Qoheleth's cosmic ethos? Standing apart from the traditions described above, creation from Qoheleth's vantage point lacks any sense of *interdependence* (cf. especially Genesis 1 and Psalm 104). The sage focuses exclusively on particular cosmic elements rather than on some grand, encompassing design: sun, wind, earth, and water are all depicted as discrete objects either locked in perpetual motion or immovably frozen, but in either case never getting anywhere. And so it is also, Qoheleth will contend, with the human being. Like the wind that blows "round and round," human beings invariably find themselves "chasing after wind," coming and going (Eccl. 1:14; 2:11, 17, 26). As the waters flow in vain to fill the sea, so human beings strive to no avail to fulfill their hopes and desires (e.g., 4:8; 6:3). And through it all, human history never changes, ever repeating itself. The cosmos, in short, reflects the crisis of the human condition as understood by this ancient sage. The cosmos is a corpus or, more accurately, a series of discrete bodies all in motion but without purpose or direction, a universe created in the image of the toiling individual. The cosmos for Qoheleth proves to be both humankind's reflection and foil in the quest for meaningful existence.

The Deadening Weight of Discourse (1:8–11)

It is no surprise, then, that Qoheleth moves effortlessly from depicting the wearying courses of the cosmos to describing the communicative faculties of the human self. The NRSV translation "all things" in verse 8 can also mean "all words." As "all things are wearisome," from the cosmic to the mundane (see above), so all language remains inadequate to express the ineffable, namely, experience itself. However plentiful, words only add to the weight of weariness. The proliferation of speech, a favorite topic of the sage, is nothing but a curse (see also 5:3, 7 [Heb. vv. 2, 6]; 6:11). For the sage, "the heavens are telling" only the absurdity of life (cf. Ps. 19:1–4). Silence, Qoheleth implies, is the only appropriate response to the weariness of it all, and yet the ear and eye are never satisfied. Like the sea they are never filled, and like ever-flowing streams human discourse continues incessantly. The *insufficiency* of discourse is matched only by the *insatiability* of the senses. As the eye and ear cannot get enough, so the mouth cannot spew out enough, unable to communicate anything of lasting value, let alone anything new.

Qoheleth's derogation of language anticipates the modernist despair over the incapacity of language to communicate perception and experience adequately, as claimed, for example, in Gustave Flaubert's *Madame Bovary* (see also Eccl. 6:11). Flaubert's image of language is that of a cackling hen or broken vessel: flat, stale, and lacking in variety (Brink, p. 130). According to Flaubert, the "heart of the tragedy of [the] human condition" lies in our being condemned to speak in a language already soiled and devalued by its prior uses (Brink, p. 139). Like Flaubert, Qoheleth claims that human discourse, like the wearisome cosmic courses, is afflicted with incessant monotony: "of making many books there is no end," notes the book's epilogist (12:12), a conclusion that is all the more true today (and applies even to Bible commentaries!).

And yet language is all we have to articulate the world. Moreover, the converse is true: the world reflects the travail of language. Like the toilsome revolutions of the cosmos, human discourse only heightens the drudgery of it all. It is as if Qoheleth denies the edifying value of any word, spoken or written. Though continually in flux, discourse is both constant and without effect (cf. Ps. 19:2). As the world turns, all discourse babbles on and history only recycles itself. Indeed, in Ecclesiastes 1:9 the sage's poetic medium becomes the message: Qoheleth repeats himself almost ad nauseum—strikingly unhebraic from a poetic standpoint—in order to underscore all the more the monotonous movements of cosmic "history." (Qoheleth, too, is trapped in the repetitive cacophony of human discourse!) The past is the future and vice versa: "there is nothing new under the sun." The poet Edna St. Vincent Millay captures well the sentiments of the ancient sage in her well-known quip: "It is not true that life is one damn thing after another—it's one damn thing over and over" (quoted from Adams, p. 205).

Qoheleth's indictment of newness, however, does serve a positive role in relation to his discourse. For all that would be considered radical and subversive about his own observations, there is nothing new, Qoheleth contends. Like Gilgamesh before him, the sage sees himself on an ancient yet perennial journey whose outcome is no different from what has been noted by those before him, namely, the finality of death

26

and the value of the ordinary (see below). The death of newness safe-guards, ironically, the veracity of Qoheleth's own discourse.

The vigor with which Qoheleth denies the existence of anything new flies in the face of that prophet of newness, the "Isaiah" of the exile:

> See, the former things have come to pass,
>   and new things I now declare;
> before they spring forth, I tell you of them.
>   (Isa. 42:9; cf. 43:18–19; 46:10; 48:7)

Perhaps Qoheleth had the prophet in mind when he rhetorically asks, "Is there a thing of which it is said, 'See, this is new'?" (v. 10a). Much is at stake over the status of newness. The apostle Paul, for example, stakes his very message on the newness that Christ brings, existentially and cos-mically: "See, everything has become new," Paul boldly proclaims (2 Cor. 5:17). Qoheleth is skeptical of such global claims. In light of the repetitive nature of history, any allegedly new thing is simply a variation of something from the past. Newness lies only in the limits of percep-tion; it is only apparent. In an age in which a new regime and socioeco-nomic order seemingly marked an unprecedented chapter in cultural history (see Introduction), the sage's assessment is a "voice of protest, reminding us that such promises of newness are a sham" (Tamez, "The Preacher," p. 25). Meaningful discourse, moreover, depends on the "new," without which human utterance is merely an exercise in monot-ony, matched only by a tiresome world devoid of wonder. And so human discourse drones on, vain as it is, while history recycles itself.

Stripped of all substance, newness is a mirage for the ancient sage. Whereas the creator is featured front and center in both Isaiah's an-nouncement of Israel's new deliverance and Paul's reflections on new life in Christ, God is strikingly absent in Qoheleth's cosmology. For Qo-heleth, the cosmos seems to move on its own frenetic inertia, ever repetitive and wearisome, with human history mirroring its lifeless movements. Social revolutions and alleged paradigm shifts are simply natural, mundane revolutions destined to be repeated time and again, but ultimately going nowhere. No progress is forthcoming: no upward and onward movement is attainable, regardless of how much energy is expended. Whatever one does, it makes no difference. Bridges built only crumble to be built again. There is no war to end all wars. Gener-ations come and go, and the wheel is ever reinvented. Like a hamster in a wheel, everything is feverishly running in place but to no avail. The cosmos is essentially stuck, frozen in time and place, despite all move-ment to the contrary. Nothing short of a dramatic intervention from God could rectify this world, "subjected to futility" in the words of Paul

27

(Rom. 8:20). Although such a possibility does not exist on the horizon of Qoheleth's purview, the ancient sage has set the stage for the world's apocalyptic encounter with God (see the epilogue of the commentary).

In addition to the illusion of newness, human history is afflicted with incurable amnesia (Eccl. 1:11). With the passing of each generation, memory is wiped clean (see also 9:5). Qoheleth is not so much claiming that human beings are utterly oblivious to the past as he is undercutting their deepest and vainglorious aspirations to secure some permanent place or "remembrance" in history. A life oriented toward ensuring its legacy for posterity only pursues the wind. The future cannot be controlled any more than the past can be fully remembered. Such a stultifying limitation on human knowledge and activity rules out all reflection about the genesis and purpose of the universe. At best, creation lies beyond the horizon of human knowledge; at worst, Qoheleth's cosmos marks the "death" of creation proper and, in turn, the demise of purposeful existence. Given the economic question introduced in 1:3 ("What do people gain . . . "), Qoheleth concludes that creation has essentially gone bust, bankrupt in the eyes of the king who would know it all.

Qoheleth, in short, renders a cosmic verdict on the meaning of human existence—indeed of all that is—and it is not positive. Human history, like the proverbial cog in the wheel, is reduced to wearisome routines. There is no "salvation history" here, no divine warrior redeeming and leading a people, let alone all creation, to some momentous consummation. No, the course of cosmic and human history is all business as usual, Qoheleth claims, and a lamentable one at that. In the exercise of living, one comes up empty-handed, as the sage will demonstrate by recounting his own vain life.

Ecclesiastes 1:12—2:26
Qoheleth's Confession: Royalty without Royalties

Now that the world according to Qoheleth has been formally introduced, the sage finally comes around to introducing himself. What follows is an autobiographical compendium of Qoheleth's royal accomplishments and experiences in what may impress modern readers as a journal of sorts, a record of personal reflections but without the expected references to particular dates. It is his testimony. Such autobiographical style is not unique to ancient literature. Choon-Leong Seow

28

has shown the obvious by arguing that the language and style of Qoheleth's self-introduction are drawn from ancient Near Eastern royal inscriptions, which typically boast of the king's accomplishments both at home and on the battlefield, the stuff of royal propaganda. But as the consummate royal sage, Qoheleth shows that he is not in the business of boasting. By adopting such language, Qoheleth in fact subverts it (Seow, *Ecclesiastes,* pp. 144–52; idem., "Qoheleth's Autobiography," pp. 257–82). As the sage overturned traditional conceptions of creation in the previous passage, so now he twists the royal testimonial into a confession of failure. And yet his royal guise is necessary for what he sets out to do. As king, Qoheleth is fully qualified to "seek and search out by wisdom" (v. 13). His royal office gives him the necessary credentials and the means to conduct his investigation.

> It is the glory of God to conceal things,
>> But the glory of kings is to search things out.
>> (Prov. 25:2)

The world is the king's classroom, his laboratory. The scope of Qoheleth's investigation covers three areas: world (1:12–15), wisdom (1:16–18; 2:12–23), and pleasure (2:1–11, 24–26).

The World's Recalcitrance (1:12–15)

The royal sage's first undertaking is to understand through wisdom "all that is done under heaven," that is, the world in all its activity under God. Wisdom (*ḥokmâ*) constitutes Qoheleth's method of investigation. Through critical observation and reflection, Qoheleth seeks to understand all worldly phenomena, both human and natural, in some unified way. Indeed, he immodestly admits that by virtue of his office and unprecedented intellectual prowess he is uniquely qualified to conduct such an investigation. As a credit to his royal glory, Qoheleth embarks on his ambitious mission to investigate all worldly phenomena and, in turn, the mind of God. Like Solomon himself, who spoke knowingly of the manifold forms of plant and animal life (1 Kings 4:33 [Heb. 5:13]), Qoheleth yearns to understand the intricate workings of nature. Like Gilgamesh, this sage aims at nothing less than understanding the totality of existence, elsewhere described as the "sum of things," an inventory of the world (Eccl. 7:25, 27). The comprehensive nature of Qoheleth's quest is matched only by the unparalleled nature of his self-perceived status as the royal sage par excellence, the one who surpasses all others in greatness (2:9). But such a noble enterprise the royal sage finds, in the end, to be eminently burdensome, an "unhappy

29

business" given by God that afflicts all human beings. As the cosmic elements go about their weary ways, so human beings are burdened with the frustrating business of making sense of their world. Though the king, above all others, possesses the means and resources to conduct such an investigation successfully, the inquiring mind is by no means unique to royalty, Qoheleth acknowledges. He is at once quintessential sage and unassuming novice in the quest for understanding. "To search out by wisdom" invites a level playing field.

Qoheleth's royal boast quickly turns into despairing lament. Indeed, the standard form of the ancient royal testimony, which showcases the mighty accomplishments of the king, becomes in Qoheleth's hands a confession of failure. For all the king's mighty efforts, the world cannot be put together in an intelligible way. There is a twistedness to reality that cannot be straightened out. Every attempt to correct leads only to a dead end. To be sure, Qoheleth has discovered something about the very nature of existence, but he finds it not worth the effort. Seeking the totality of things is nothing more than "chasing after wind" (1:14). Therein lies a paradox: Qoheleth, in his global ambition to understand "all," has arrived at the conclusion that "all is vanity" (see also v. 2). As king—the earthly counterpart to divinity in ancient Near Eastern tradition—Qoheleth is able to grasp something of the totality of existence but not in any satisfying or meaningful way. Indeed, his quest has made him a fool, for only fools pursue the wind (cf. Hos. 12:1; Sir. 34:1–2).

What did Qoheleth expect? As the proverb cited in Ecclesiastes 1:15 illustrates, Qoheleth hoped to make intelligible sense of the world. Instead, he found only "crookedness," a world intractably resistant to the intellectual prowess of the king (see also 7:13). The royal sage wields a rather sophisticated view of epistemology: to understand something is to construct meaningful coherence of experience. To understand is to create sense out of chaos. Wisdom is no passive instrument; indeed, it can be a powerful tool, especially in royal hands, for making sense of the world. Yet the legendary king has met his match. This gnarled world remains impervious to Qoheleth's intellectual efforts (cf. 1:4b). It remains devoid of purposeful meaning. Like the sand on the seashore or the innumerable stars in the heavens, the world's deficiency cannot be measured (v. 15b). This proverb, the language of which the sages used to describe their recalcitrant students, Qoheleth applies to the world as a whole. The universe, in effect, is hopelessly stubborn; it cannot be molded to correspond to any human models of moral sense and order. To understand the world is to impose a *sensible* order upon it; but the world invariably frustrates any and all attempts.

30

Qoheleth has indeed found a worldly, albeit frustrating, coherence, but its veracity cannot satisfy his intellectual longings. By concluding that "all is vanity," Qoheleth has come to know the world as alien and himself as a stranger in it.

The Folly of Wisdom (1:16–18)

Having found the totality of activity wanting, Qoheleth turns on wisdom itself. Boasting in standard royal hyperbole ("surpassing all [plural!] who were over Jerusalem before me" [see also 2:7, 9]), this king of kings claims to have accumulated an unprecedented amount of wisdom (see 1 Kings 10:7, 23). Wisdom is something he knows intimately; thus, he is supremely qualified to continue his investigation, this time of wisdom and folly, the polar opposites that comprise the totality of human thought and conduct. Yet, frustrated again, he finds scarcely any difference between the two. Whereas "vexation" is intimately related to foolish behavior, either as cause or result (e.g., Prov. 12:16; 17:25; 27:3), Qoheleth finds it to be, in fact, a product of wisdom. Conventional wisdom, as reflected in much of the book of Proverbs, contends that the pursuit of wisdom guarantees happiness and prosperity (e.g., Prov. 2:10; 3:13–18), and those who would succumb to folly will only find grief, if not self-ruin (Prov. 5:9–14; cf. Eccl. 7:17). Qoheleth, however, observes that the misfortunes of folly apply also to wisdom! Such a conclusion is tantamount to sapiential blasphemy, which the sage, as a master of irony, casts in the classic form of a proverb. Qoheleth has turned wisdom against itself. Paul in effect converts Qoheleth's lament into a basis for praise when he boasts of God's foolishness as "wiser than human wisdom" (1 Cor. 1:18–25; see the epilogue of the commentary).

Of Royal Perks and Parks: The Vanity of Pleasure (2:1–11)

Next, Qoheleth conducts a "test" of pleasure or enjoyment, although his "test" involves not so much a trial as a critical inquiry into the enduring value of pleasure. But before the sage tabulates the results of his investigation, he pronounces at the outset his verdict: "vanity." Laughter and joy ultimately prove deficient (Eccl. 2:2). How Qoheleth gets from the topic of his inquiry to such a damning judgment is described in verses 3–10, in which the king details his work in investigating pleasure. The sage presents his work as his royal résumé. Therein Qoheleth itemizes his accomplishments for the purpose of discerning

31

"what was good for mortals . . . during the few days of their life" (v. 3). With wisdom as his guide, Qoheleth accomplishes great things in his pursuit of pleasure, from erecting monumental buildings to amassing great wealth and cultivating the "delights of the flesh." With the exception of this last entry, Qoheleth's account draws from the stock language employed by ancient Near Eastern despots, language that Qoheleth exposes as the cacophony of conceit.

Much of Qoheleth's attention, for example, is devoted to the cultivation of gardens (vv. 4–6). In addition to boasting of their physical prowess tested on the battlefield and hunting expeditions, the kings of the ancient Orient also took pride in their horticultural skills at home, exemplified by their resplendent palace gardens, a practice continued, for example, by many European kings in modern history (e.g., Louis XIV [1643–1715 A.D.] at Versailles). Any king worth his salt had to excel in handling the sword in one hand and the garden spade in the other. The cultivation of arid land for human settlement was of particular importance to kings, for it advanced the claim of the monarchy against raw nature, as well as symbolically furthered the king's claim over foreign territories. Indeed, both Egyptian and Mesopotamian rulers frequently boasted of having cultivated certain botanical species from the foreign lands they had conquered, claiming that these transplants flourished better in their own gardens than in their native environments. Such gardens were literally "victory gardens"! (See Brown, *The Ethos of the Cosmos,* pp. 248–52.) In addition, it is worth noting that the primordial Garden of 'ēden ("delight") in Genesis 2—3 is most likely modeled after the royal pleasure garden (see "the King's Garden" in 2 Kings 25:4; Jer. 39:4; Neh. 3:15). Indeed, the garden, whether real or imaginary, was regarded as a scene for lovemaking (Cant. 4:11—5:2; cf. Gen. 2:23—25).

The king's green thumb, in short, demonstrated his prowess in mastering nature and extending, symbolically, his realm, as well as his voracity for pleasure. Whether in monumental construction, horticulture, or sex, "Do it in unmatchable excess!" was the motto for many an ancient (and modern) autocrat. By his accomplishments, Qoheleth the king hopes to achieve unsurpassed heroic status vis-à-vis his predecessors and successors, indeed all mortals. By dint of royal might, Qoheleth recreates the garden in the pursuit of happiness and virtual immortality through a hero's enduring fame and glory (see 2:16; cf. the discussion of Gilgamesh in the Introduction). Although the pursuit of pleasure has its challenges, requiring great toil, Qoheleth conducts it with alacrity, for he hopes to achieve nothing short of his apotheosis.

Such a pursuit, the sage makes clear, is conducted with wisdom (2:3, 9). Throwing restraint, but not prudence, to the wind, the king claims that he has "found pleasure in [literally 'from'] all my toil" (v. 10). Although the world cannot be straightened out or wisdom found fully satisfying, Qoheleth does experience a measure of pleasure from his grand accomplishments. Delight is his "reward" (NRSV), literally his "lot" or "portion." It is to be distinguished from profit or "gain" (2:11b). Yet it all crumbles in his hands, all his accomplishments as well as his toil in achieving them (v. 11). The shift from pride in accomplishment to disillusionment in verse 11 is abrupt. The verb that begins his critical assessment literally means "I turned" or "faced" (*pānâ*). Having sought self-glorification through his accomplishments, Qoheleth must now face the facts of his finitude. Like Gilgamesh, he takes account of his vast achievements and the prodigious energy required in accomplishing them and finds that he has come up empty-handed. He must face the question the wise Utanapishtim throws at Gilgamesh: "You have toiled without cease, and what have you got?" (see Introduction). But unlike Gilgamesh, who in the end found fulfillment in the great walls of Uruk which he had built, Qoheleth finds his monuments to the self devoid of enduring value.

It is here that the despairing king directly addresses the question posed back in 1:3: "What do people gain from all the toil . . . ?" His answer leaves no wiggle room: "There is *nothing* to be gained under the sun" (2:11b). Even through his unparalleled accomplishments, Qoheleth could find no gain, no lasting legacy to crown his prodigious efforts. Like a mirage, what appeared to be a genuine, enduring good for mortals, namely, gain achieved through monumental labor, is found wanting when critically assayed for its enduring worth. All that is left is the joy of the toil (v. 10), fleeting and inefficacious, but, as Qoheleth will later discern, close to redemptive (vv. 24–26). For the time being, at least, the royal sage has again found himself chasing the wind (v. 11a), an insanely foolish enterprise (see Prov. 12:11b). What provokes Qoheleth to see his achievements disappear in a puff of smoke is, however, not readily identified. The reason for his negative assessment is not fully explicated until the following section.

At this point, it may seem ludicrous to go any further in exploring Qoheleth's thought, particularly from a Christian context. The ancient sage's verdict that absolutely nothing in life is gainful, that all is vanity, would appear to contravene the very ethos of faith. Yet, as an indispensable part of the canon, Ecclesiastes actually lays the groundwork for specifically Christian theological reflection and conduct. It is striking, for example, that Paul, like Qoheleth, recounts with pride his lifelong accomplishments, boasting of his unmatched zeal as a blameless follower of the law (Phil. 3:4–6). Paul avers that his "confidence in the flesh" surpasses all others. Nevertheless, the apostle counts it all for

33

nothing: "whatever gains I had, these I have come to regard as loss" (v. 7; cf. Eccl. 2:11). All "rubbish" (or more literally "shit" [Greek *skubalon*]) is Paul's indictment against his self-made, self-righteous life, fashioned through obedience to the Torah, to which Qoheleth would add, "all *hebel*" (Phil. 3:8; Eccl. 1:2; 2:11). For both the apostle and the sage, there is a gift, given by God to be received but is by no means possessed. For Paul, that gift is Christ, who imparts a righteousness that is not his own (Phil. 3:8–9). For Qoheleth, it is the simple yet fleeting gift of pleasure that is found in the toil yet is not of his own making (see Eccl. 2:24–26). This is not the pleasure for which one strives heroically but the pleasure of the ordinary which one receives, gratuitously extended by God. Discerning how these gifts of God relate, of Christ on the one hand and delight on the other, is the fruitful challenge of understanding Qoheleth theologically (see the epilogue of the commentary). And it begins by recognizing the sublime within the *hebel*.

Death and the Demise of Wisdom (2:12–23)

Giving up on pleasure, for the time being at least, Qoheleth turns again to examine wisdom and folly (see 1:17–18), but now his purview is widened beyond the scope of his own life as king (2:12). In context, the royal sage's declaration in verse 12b that no one can exceed what the king has already done is more a lament than a boast. If the king cannot achieve something of enduring value, then no one who comes after him can. If only something new could be accomplished! But no. Having found that the excessive royal lifestyle brings no sense of lasting fulfillment, Qoheleth broadens his scope and examines his legacy for posterity. By lining up wisdom and folly side by side Qoheleth finds encouraging that wisdom appears to yield *relative* advantage or profit, contrary to his earlier assessment in 2:11. The contrast is stark: whereas wisdom is the source of enlightened discernment, folly is rooted in darkness. Verse 14a is typical of proverbial wisdom, which frequently delineates an absolute contrast between the sage and the fool or wicked (e.g., Prov. 10:1, 8, 21, 23; 15:7). Regarding the metaphors of light and darkness, one finds similar usage in the following comparison:

> The path of the righteous is like the light of dawn,
>> which shines brighter and brighter until full day.
> The way of the wicked is like deep darkness;
>> they do not know what they stumble over.
>> (Prov. 4:18–19)

In addition to denoting intelligence, light connotes life, whereas darkness suggests ignorance and death (Job 17:12–16; 18:18; Isa. 9:2 [Heb.

v. 1]; John 1:5; 3:19–21; 12:35–36a; 1 John 1:6–7; 2:8–11). In conventional wisdom, a hard and fast distinction between the wise and the fool's demise is established. "Fools die for lack of sense," while righteousness, wisdom's cardinal virtue, "delivers from death," that is, from an untimely one (Prov. 10:2b, 21b; 11:4b). With typical poetic hyperbole, the sages boldly asserted that wisdom is a "tree of life," recalling the arbor of Eden that was barred from Adam's grasp (Prov. 3:16; Gen. 3:22–23).

For Qoheleth, however, the tree has withered and died. The seemingly black-and-white contrast between wisdom and folly dissolves into a sea of gray before the indiscriminate reality of death. Whether sage or fool, king or commoner, all must succumb to the great equalizer and cross the threshold into the democracy of the dead. "Why," Qoheleth asks himself, "did I excel in wisdom?" Qoheleth the king had hoped to be wisdom's champion. Instead, like Gilgamesh, he found himself defeated, powerless before death, the ultimate assayer. Wisdom, too, is a mirage, promising a life of blessing and purpose but delivering only vanity and vexation (1:18).

But, one may ask, what did this sage expect? Even amid his greatest expectations, Qoheleth never once thought that he could actually escape the clutches of death, which Gilgamesh vainly attempted to do (see Introduction). As for what he personally desired, a clear answer is given in verse 16. The ultimate desire that even wisdom and pleasure cannot satisfy is the desire for *remembrance*. With deliverance from death out of the question, Qoheleth's expectations rest on securing an enduring memory of his reputation, the next best thing to immortality. Like the builders of Babel, Qoheleth wanted to establish his name for all generations through his innumerable accomplishments. But death, he observes, marks not only the cessation of life but also the dissolution of collective memory. Every generation comes and goes, and the past is utterly forgotten (see 1:4, 11). Yet a wholly unanticipated (?) irony emerges from this passage in relation to the whole. As the walls of Uruk (and an epic tale) were meant to preserve remembrance of Gilgamesh for future generations, a small and unassuming book has become Qoheleth's lasting legacy.

Qoheleth had hoped that the wise would experience a fate qualitatively, if not quantitatively, different from the fate of the foolish. To be sure, death cannot be evaded, but the removal of a wise person's name and reputation from collective human memory, comparable to the deserving fate of the fool, is in Qoheleth's eyes nothing short of a travesty of justice. What Qoheleth finds particularly disturbing is having to give up all that he worked for with tremendous effort and ingenuity, leaving it to the whims of undeserving successors (vv. 19, 21), like casting pearls before swine. This sage's dismay matches Enkidu's rage against the doorway he had carefully constructed only to leave it to Gilgamesh to possess and use after his death (see Introduction). Ownership and honor cut to the heart of the matter: Qoheleth can no more control the fate of his reputation and the legacy of his labors—his "lot" (v. 21)—than he can resuscitate himself after death, a grave travesty, this *hebel*. The erstwhile master of abundance must relinquish his claim over all that he has upon death, leaving the fruits and legacies of his labors for successive generations to waste and abuse.

Qoheleth the sage is not alone in this all-consuming concern. Preserving a legacy for posterity was of utmost concern to most ancient despots. A typical element of the royal memorial, which gave codified witness to the mighty works of the king, was the final warning addressed to any who would dare to efface the king's testimonial inscription, invoking even the gods of disease and death as a deterrent. Messing with a predecessor's royal résumé and monumental testimonies was considered anathema, at least by the deceased king, warranting judgment and curse. Yet that did not prevent royal claimants to the throne, particularly usurpers, from effacing the glorious testimonies of their predecessors in order to highlight their own accomplishments. The systematic effacement, for example, of the engraved depictions and inscriptions of the female pharaoh Hatchepsut (1498–1483 B.C.) by her nephew and successor Thutmosis III (1504–1450 B.C.) is but one instance of the political ruination of the past. *C'est la vie royal.*

In the face of such future uncertainty, Qoheleth is wracked by despair over his present life, disillusioned with all that he has accomplished. He is concerned not only about the preservation of his royal glory for posterity but also about the devolution of inherited property. The sage laments that he has absolutely no say over who will end up controlling his property once he dies. Indeed, both of Qoheleth's concerns—his reputation and possessions—are intertwined, since one's property, land in particular, was for Israel inextricably tied to one's familial identity and thus was kept from one generation to the next within the family. The story of Naboth's vineyard, in which King Ahab illicitly annexes Naboth's ancestral inheritance, dramatically illustrates the land's integral role in the communal life of ancient Israel (1 Kings 21:1–16; see the discussion of Eccl. 5:9).

Like property, a person's reputation is passed on to and preserved by posterity. If one's self-consuming labors cannot cultivate a venerable legacy for future generations, then it is all for nothing, Qoheleth concludes. The pain and vexation involved in such toil simply add insult to injury. Work has become a monstrous affliction, devoid of any payoff yet insidiously invading even the bliss of nocturnal rest, the curse of sabbathless existence. Although all consuming, toil is irredeemably bankrupt, amounting to nothing more than an exercise in vanity (v. 23; see v. 1). Yet all is not lost. There remains something redemptive that makes life still worth living despite the vanity of toil, but it can be realized—or more accurately received—only when all hope for self-achievement and glory is surrendered. Such is the lesson of death.

The Vestiges of Joy (2:24–26)

Qoheleth concludes his investigation on a modestly upbeat note (vv. 24–26). With all hope for enduring remembrance sacrificed upon the altar of uncertainty (v. 16), something nonetheless remains, namely, the simple pleasures of eating, drinking, and, literally, "seeing good in one's work." These are the vestiges of joy, and yet they are emblematic of civilized culture (see the account of Enkidu's acculturation in the Introduction). Seven times Qoheleth acknowledges or commends enjoyment in various forms (2:24–26; 3:12–13, 22; 5:18–20; 8:15; 9:7–10; 11:9–10). Common to them all is the utter lack of self-pretension, ambition, or obsession. These minimal "goods" are purged by death and life's vicissitudes of all illusions of grandeur that had characterized Qoheleth's "monumental phase" (2:4–11), when pleasure was considered a lasting gain to be wrested *from* one's toil for the means of self-glorification (vv. 9–10).

As Qoheleth comes to realize, joy is not a means to a greater, vainglorious end. The true pleasures are the most mundane. They are the "simple gifts." Whereas Qoheleth found his life in a constant state of ceaseless activity and accomplishment, of making, building, planting, and gathering (vv. 4–8)—the all-consuming and self-aggrandizing labors of any oriental despot—he now discovers what is ultimately worthwhile: the task of *receiving*. Neither achieved nor planned, neither grasped nor produced, the gifts of true pleasure are simply received from God. Indeed, there is no other way, for even the capacity for enjoyment is God-given (v. 25). Like the "stranger" who arbitrarily transfers the fruits of one person's labor to someone undeserving (v. 21; 6:2), God freely gives the benefits of wisdom, knowledge, and joy (2:26). But unlike the "stranger," God's inscrutability lies in a perverse magnanimity to the "one who is good."

As eating and drinking exemplify the simple pleasures of sustenance, received in gratitude and savored for their own sake, they are also fraught with much background in sapiential rhetoric. In

37

conventional wisdom, the partaking of food and drink typically signifies the appropriation of wisdom. Of the many roles assumed by personified wisdom in Proverbs 1—9, from prophet to playful child, most striking is her role as consummate hostess, serving wine and meat to her disciples in the sapiential banquet, the feast of insight (Prov. 9:1–6). "Does not the ear test words as the palate tastes food?" asks Job in assessing his friends' unappreciated advice (Job 12:11). In sapiential discourse, there is much food for thought and table talk to be digested. It is no surprise, then, that for Qoheleth "wisdom, knowledge, and joy" are part of a single package that also includes the delights of taste and simple sustenance, all tied together with a bow, as a gift to those whom God favors (Eccl. 2:26a). "O taste and see that the Lord is good," the psalmist proclaims (Ps. 34:8).

The third pleasure that Qoheleth mentions in his taxonomy of joy—enjoyment in one's work—requires nothing less than a change of perception or attitude ("see") about the very nature of work (see the epilogue of the commentary). Work as a means to a greater end or gain, such as lasting fame, security, or even pleasure, results only in frustration and disillusionment (v. 23), as Qoheleth has demonstrated in his own life. But work enjoyed in and of itself is what Qoheleth has come to value, particularly in light of his royal failure to guarantee an "enduring remembrance." No longer is enjoyment to be *gained from* one's toil (v. 10); it is recognized as part and parcel of one's work, *discerned within* the labor, an intrinsic joy (v. 24). Although death undercuts the ambition to achieve permanence of identity, it cannot vanquish the enjoyment of the moment. Indeed, death serves to set such joy in starker relief.

In contrast to the indiscriminate swath of death's sickle, joy is discriminately given by God. Qoheleth contrasts the recipient of joy, who pleases God, and the sinner, who is burdened with the task of "gathering and heaping," yet whose gains are then given to those who enjoy God's favor (cf. Prov. 13:22). The irony, as Seow points out, is that Qoheleth, apropos to his name, is himself a "gatherer" (Seow, *Ecclesiastes*, p. 158). Although a clear distinction is made between the deserving recipient and the sinner, it also presents something of a quandary. God alone determines the moral mettle of the self, and Qoheleth finds himself impaled on the horns of an existential dilemma: the sage is both a gatherer and a recipient. The phenomenon of joy, thus, offers only a partial resolution while heightening the impenetrable mystery of life granted by an inscrutable God. But rather than obsessively trying to fathom the mystery as if it were a problem to be solved, Qoheleth comes to appreciate life on its own terms. He begins by acknowledging the irresistible power of death and, thereby, the fleeting yet profoundly redemptive moments of joy amid the toil. As anyone who has suffered senseless tragedy knows, coming to terms is in itself quite an achievement. By coming to terms with absurdity, Qoheleth is able to discern the sublime within the mundane and the glory within the ordinary.

Qoheleth's commendation of joy is no different from the advice given to Saul by the "medium at Endor" on the night before the king was to die in battle (1 Sam. 28:3–25). Having heard the spirit of Samuel proclaim his death, the doomed king falls to the ground, paralyzed with fear.

> The woman came to Saul, and when she saw that he was terrified, she said to him, "Your servant has listened to you. . . . Now therefore, you also listen to your servant; let me set a morsel of bread before you. Eat, that you may have strength when you go on your way." He refused, and said, "I will not eat." But his servants, together with the woman, urged him; and he listened to their words. So he got up from the ground and sat on the bed. Now the woman had a fatted calf in the house. She quickly slaughtered it, and she took flour, kneaded it, and baked unleavened cakes. She put them before Saul and his servants, and they ate. Then they rose and went away that night. (vv. 21–25)

The Deuteronomist describes in intimate detail the care with which the woman ministered to the incapacitated king. This "witch" of Endor offers a moment of sustenance, a pause for dignity, to Saul in his descent into the valley of death's shadow. And then there is Jephthah's daughter, who accepts with dignity her unjust death, brought about by her father's rash vow. Resisting the paralysis of death, she takes matters into her own hands and founds a new community, a fellowship of lament that would continue after her death (Judg. 11:37–39). And, of course, there is Jesus, whose last supper on the eve of his death was not without the poignant joy of fellowship (Matt. 26:29–30). We are all, Qoheleth suggests, like Saul and Jephthah's daughter, whose next meal may be our last. From the day we are born we are doomed to die, absurdly so. But the ancient sage urges us to continue on our way, into the night if need be, on the journey toward death . . . and joy.

Regarding his initial observations of the cosmos (Eccl. 1:8–11), the somber sage has come to notice amid the sun's wearisome circuits across the sky those occasional sunrises and sunsets that for the briefest of moments inflame the skies with brilliant radiance, captivating those who have the eyes to behold them (see 11:7; 12:2). But with every sunset, however resplendent, darkness falls, and with every dawn comes the "toil under the sun." Moving from global weariness to fleeting joy, Qoheleth has found God-given redemption in the details of a vain life, his own and all humanity's.

39

Ecclesiastes 3:1–22
Chronology without History

Arguably the most well-known passage in the book, Ecclesiastes
3:1–8 maintains its appeal in popular culture. Many readers, particularly those in the so-called Baby Boomer generation, cannot hear the
first verse without mentally humming the musical version by Pete
Seeger, "Turn! Turn! Turn!," which the Byrds made famous with their
recording in the mid–1960s. This discrete unit stands out as a poetic
gem in a seemingly otherwise dark and convoluted book. Indeed, Qoheleth himself may have adopted it rather than composed it *de novo,* to
which he adds his theological commentary in verses 9–22. In any case,
this poem about time and the polarities of human activity is a source of
both disillusionment and awe, as one also finds in the sage's description
of the cosmos that prefaces his deliberations (1:3–8).

These verses form the chronological counterpart to Qoheleth's
cosmology. Both poems capture the nature of existence in its rawest,
most limiting, and yet all-encompassing form. The former is characterized by space and movement, a *cosmos* without *protos* or purposeful beginning; the latter deals with time and determination in the human
realm, a chronology without progression or history, *chronos* without *telos* (see 1:10). As the wind and sun are ever locked in their incessant cir-
cumambulations, so human activity is forever oscillating from one
extreme to the other, from sorrow to celebration, from building up to
tearing down, and vice versa. To match the circuitous movements of the
cosmos, Qoheleth depicts the incessant oscillations that characterize
the passing of time. As 1:9 serves as the conclusion to Qoheleth's cosmology, so 3:15, parallel in meaning, concludes his reflections on
chronology. Like streams flowing into the sea, time is ever in flux, devoid of progress or constancy. Both time and space lack the stability to
ensure purposeful existence, an awareness most keenly felt by today's
so-called Generation X (see Beaudoin, pp. 127–29).

The Poetry of Polarity (3:1–8)

40   Qoheleth provides the thesis statement of this unit at the outset:
every event has its time or season. A catalogue of contrasting moments
follows, vividly illustrating his thesis: twenty-eight items in a series of

fourteen temporal antimonies. Poetically, these pairs of opposites serve as poetic *merisms;* they convey a sense of the totality of human endeavor in all its manifold forms. Scholars have labored hard to discern some kind of systematic structure, but to no avail. Yet the series is no mere hodge-podge of contrasting moments. The first line refers to birth and death (v. 2), and the last mentions war and peace (v. 8), forming an envelope of ultimacy. Within this poetic bracket, the catalog covers a gamut of contrasting human activities: for example, planting and plucking, killing and restoring, construction and demolition, sorrow and celebration, tearing and mending, love and hatred, silence and utterance. No particular order of appearance is evident. Moreover, the particular significance of at least one of the items remains elusive to modern readers: throwing and gathering stones in v. 5 (a game, land cultivation, or sexual activity?).

What is clear, however, is that both the desiderata and the detestable have their "place" in the chronological circumference of human existence. No preference is given to either one or the other. Furthermore, what may appear undesirable on one occasion might be appropriate for another. Qoheleth is no idealist, optimistically calling forth a time of peace and celebration that can erase the less desirable dimensions of human existence. Rather, the sage calmly observes that for every course of action in one direction, there will occur in due time an equal and opposite reaction. If the cosmos operates like clockwork, impersonal and repetitive, then *chronos* is its pendulum, held aloft by God. Each activity, whether positive or negative, has its season, and the seasons themselves have their place in the rhythm of the ever-circling years. Dancing, for example, is not appropriate during mourning. Weeping is out of sync with celebrations. Silence is not golden when the rights of the oppressed are at stake (cf. 4:1). Even hatred has its time, as demonstrated in the psalms that imprecate unnamed enemies (e.g., Pss. 58:6–11; 137:7–9; 139:19–22; cf. Eccl. 2:18). Each activity has its relative worth and suitability, its "place" in the grand providential scheme. But no one activity has universal sway any more than exhaling or inhaling dominates the rhythm of breathing. Permanence is not part of the chronological equation. The poetic arrangement of these moments suggests that such opposites are actually counterparts, all part and parcel of the temporal rhythm of life, which never progresses yet never stops.

So far, Qoheleth's vision of time does not stray far from the tenets of conventional wisdom, whose message frequently is not so much "know thyself" as "know thy time," particularly in matters of speech and conduct:

> To make an apt answer is a joy to anyone,
>   and a word in season, how good it is!
>   (Prov. 15:23)

41

> A word fitly spoken is like apples of gold in a setting of silver.
> (Prov. 25:11)

> [There is] a time to keep silence, and a time to speak.
> (Eccl. 3:7b)

Analogous to the priestly task of determining the spatial separations between the sacred and the profane (see Lev. 10:10–11; Ezek. 44:23), the sage's mission is to discern the right and wrong time for appropriate conduct and speech. Giving an "answer before hearing," for example, is tantamount to folly (Prov. 18:13). To master life is in part to determine when (and what or whom) to embrace and when to refrain. Indeed, a form of situational ethics is espoused in Prov. 26:4–5, which provides two contradictory modes of conduct before the fool:

> Do not answer fools according to their folly,
> or you will be a fool yourself,

> Answer fools according to their folly,
> or they will be wise in their own eyes.

Both proverbs are adamant in their directives, and each offers a legitimate rationale for prescribing a particular course of action. But together they constitute an unmitigated contradiction! It is left to the wise reader to discern the situation and decide how to act. There is a time to respond and a time to remain silent. Such concern for conduct appropriate to its time underlies Qoheleth's poetic catalog.

The Suitability of Mystery (3:9–15)

In light of the prose commentary that follows (vv. 9–15), significant differences emerge between Qoheleth's presentation of the times and the insights of conventional wisdom. Even though humanity is the grammatical subject of the various infinitives—*people* plant and pluck up, mourn and dance—the human subject is by no means the determiner of such events. Qoheleth makes clear that God alone is the one who determines; God is the primary, albeit implicit, actor on the temporal scene. The ever-constant swings of time's pendulum are suspended and held firmly by God. The nature of God's determinations from Qoheleth's perspective can be compared with conventional wisdom:

> The Lord has made everything for its purpose. . . .
> (Prov. 16:4a)

42

> God has made everything suitable for its time; . . .
> (Eccl. 3:11a)

It may seem that both statements are fully compatible, if not identical, in meaning. Yet appearances are deceiving. The slight change in terminology betrays the decisive difference. To be sure, both statements claim God's unsurpassable sovereignty in and over creation. From Qoheleth's perspective, God's determinations are immutably sufficient; nothing can be added or subtracted from them (v. 14; cf. Prov. 30:5–6). God's determinations are unchangeable; human action is ineffectual. But whereas conventional wisdom affirms that God has a discernible "purpose" (literally "answer" [*ma'ǎneh*]) for everything created, as in the case of the wicked's demise, Qoheleth describes God's will much more modestly: everything is created "suitable for its time." More sharply, nowhere does Qoheleth talk explicitly about purposefulness in the created order or in history, for that would assume discernible direction and eventual consummation in the course of human affairs, which he finds absolutely lacking. Any intimation of linear progression in the created order is utterly beyond human grasp, although the yearning for such direction is ever present (v. 11b). Rather, like the wearisome revolutions of the sun and the wind, time continually recycles itself, oscillating between the opposite poles of human activity. There is no real history, only chronic reversals. Concerning every event, for weal or for woe, one can only say resignedly in one moment and hopeful in the next, "This too shall pass."

What then is humanity's role? As in Qoheleth's previous reflections, people are not so much the shapers as the recipients of life. First and foremost, human beings are preoccupied with toil as part of their God-given lot in life. Although they must earn their bread by the sweat of their brow, they accomplish nothing that is enduring, Qoheleth observes, except at most their own subsistence. Once again, the issue of "gain" is broached (3:9; cf. 1:3; 2:11). In a state of existence that is characterized by the recycling of human activity, the matter of gain is a non sequitur. Humans are afflicted with busy-ness, scarcely aimless but never gainful. There is something "suitable" to every kind of activity, although it cannot be fully grasped by the human intellect. Such suitability is glimpsed, however meagerly, only by the God-given capacity to sense the eternal: "[God] has put a sense of past and future (literally 'eternity') into their minds" (v. 11). Human beings are endowed with the facility to step back from immediate situations and particular events that vie for their attention to catch a glimpse of the totality of existence, including their own. Such is the mark of self-consciousness. Yet they remain ignorant of any purposeful providence that underlies the totality, "from the beginning to the end." Human beings, in short, are caught between self-transcendence and stifling ignorance. They are both in time and out of time.

The capacity to step back and view the totality of one's existence, as theologians and ethicists point out, is necessary for moral living, and Qoheleth does not deny this (Brown, *Character in Crisis,* pp. 132–33). The capacity to transcend oneself, in fact, points to the conundrum of human existence for Qoheleth. Human beings are endowed with the capacity to look beyond the immediacy of life, to suspend oneself, however delicately, above the fray to sense the eternal but are never quite able to grasp the meaning of it all.

Though by no means an exhaustive catalogue, Qoheleth's poetic list of human occasions attests the encompassing scope of human perception and cognition. The poem, moreover, lends poignant elegance to the series of harsh polarities that characterize human activity. Qoheleth's view of the suitability of the times does not lack in "beauty"—RSV's translation of *yâpeh* in v. 11—or aesthetic balance. Yet it does not, indeed cannot, indicate any overarching plan or direction, the perceived lack of which is a source of perennial frustration for human beings, Qoheleth observes. Sensing the eternal and toiling with life's contingencies are part of the human condition, allotted by God (vv. 10, 11bα). Any understanding of divine providence resides solely with the eternal subject. Any actual history of human existence, as providentially configured, remains a mystery. Even though the human intellect cannot grasp the divine method behind the structured madness of human activity, God nonetheless grants a sense of the eternal to human beings. Yet this sixth sense, as it were, does not enable the human subject to discern even intimations of divine providence. There is, thus, a dark side to this enlightened sense, the sense of the eternal. Human beings can only glimpse, but never grasp, the course of human affairs, much less control them. It is within this state of betwixt and between that human beings must continue to toil to make some sense of life under the sun, subsisting only on traces of the eternal.

Qoheleth's portrayal of time bears significant implications for human existence. The sage acknowledges subtly sublime moments of *kairos* embedded within this monotonous *chronos.* Although human beings are burdened with the task of toiling, they are also given certain occasions of joy: the simple gifts of eating, drinking, and enjoying one's work (see 2:24). Moreover, the times for building, embracing, and loving are integral moments in a person's life; they cannot be denied. In them, eternity encounters the contingent particularities of life, setting in sharp relief those fleeting moments that impart pleasure and awe, purpose and fulfillment, to an otherwise empty existence. As God gives busy-ness, God also gives precious moments of joy amid the busy-ness. Such pleasures must not be taken lightly, either by denying them their rightful place in the rhythms of life or by taking them for granted, overlooked in the pursuit of the future. Only the present moment, Qoheleth contends, can endow human existence with any sense of meaning. Only in the present lies a glimmer of the eternal.

Qoheleth boldly states that God's sufficiency in human affairs is intended to provoke awe (literally "fear") before the divine (v. 14). Terror, surely, is not what Qoheleth means, contrary to common opinion. Qoheleth does not depict God as a divine "Terminator," targeting humanity with unrelieved oppression, as depicted in Job's bitter protestations (e.g., Job 6:4; 7:17–21; 9:17–19; 16:14). God is not a divine tyrant intent on frightening people. Qoheleth is no Job, that master of malediction, any more than God is a "cosmic bully" who wages war against creation. The ancient sage does not lash out against his inscrutable, omnipotent Creator as the whale hunter Ahab does against his formidable prey in Herman Melville's classic: "He tasks me; he heaps me; I see in him outrageous strength, with an inscrutable malice sinewing it. That inscrutable thing is chiefly what I hate" (*Moby Dick*, chapter 36, p. 236). For Qoheleth, the "fear of God" is more a moral realization than a sensation of dread or outrage before the deity. Reverence of God is founded upon an acute awareness of one's finitude vis-à-vis God, wholly Other and wholly sovereign. "God is in heaven, and you upon earth," Qoheleth observes in 5:2 (Heb. v. 1). Awe is the appropriate response to the *mysterium tremendum,* but not to any despot who provokes only terror or defiance.

For Qoheleth, an awareness of the systemic limitations of human existence is fundamental to cultivating awe of God. Only God creates with perdurability (3:14), surpassing anything human beings—including even a king at the height of his power—can achieve. Sovereignty rests upon the unalterable sufficiency of divine purpose, inscrutable though it is. Despite the diverse and disparate forms of human activity limned so elegantly in verses 1–8, the one thing that human beings can*not* do is add to or subtract from what God has done (v. 14). The past cannot be retracted or augmented. (Qoheleth is no historical revisionist!) What is more, reverence to God includes a posture of gratitude for the pleasures gratuitously imparted by God to human beings, including pleasure *in* the very task of toiling (cf. 9:10).

The final verse offers a fitting, albeit enigmatic, conclusion to Qoheleth's meditation on the life and times of human activity. Repeating an earlier sentiment, the sage observes the repetitiveness of "history," which had led him to disclaim all notions of anything *new*sworthy (1:9). But whereas Qoheleth's cosmological meditations make no reference to the deity, the sage refers to God in 3:15: "God seeks out what has gone by" (literally, "what is pursued"). On one level, such a statement claims God as the prime recycler of history, "seeking out" the past only

45

to repeat it. Yet the careful choice of language suggests something more. The exegetical crux is found in the disputed meaning of the last term, literally "pursued" (*nirdap*), which is nowhere else attested in Ecclesiastes. Yet Qoheleth frequently refers to ill-fated human endeavors to achieve something but without success. "The race is not to the swift, nor the battle to the strong, nor bread to the wise," observes Qoheleth (9:11a). Conversely, no one can anticipate the time of calamity, which can ruin the best-laid plans (9:12).

As Seow points out, "what is pursued" in 3:15 likely refers to "that which people seek in vain," tantamount to pursuing the wind (Seow, *Ecclesiastes,* p. 166). That does not thereby mean, however, that "God will look after what people have pursued in vain." The syntax, rather, highlights divine activity *over and against* human activity. Only God successfully seeks out and apprehends whatever is sought (by God or human being). Only God determines the result, such as who will win the battle, who will receive another's gain, and who will succeed (cf. Prov. 16:1, 9; 21:31). Qoheleth has seen too much failure and tragedy as the result of good intentions and hard work. The bottom line for the sage is that the gain for which one toils invariably slips through the fingers or turns against the toiler. Qoheleth has also seen wickedness evict justice and righteousness from their rightful place (Eccl. 3:16). Even there a divine method lies behind the madness of it all.

The Pedagogy of Wickedness (3:16–22)

The language of Qoheleth's reflections shifts from temporal to spatial references. The sage finds wickedness "in the place of" righteousness and justice, comparable to corruption in the court of law and depravity in the soul of society. Although nothing new, such moral displacement is clearly out of bounds for the sage who has seen it all (cf. 4:1; 5:8; 8:11; 9:3). Whereas time in its oscillating rhythms is characterized by suitability, determined by God, moral space is violated. Wickedness is out of place. Resolution for the sage lies in God's providential yet inscrutable timing as a way of rectifying the dislocation of justice. Specifically, the sage calls for divine retribution, since every deed has its time in God's determination (v. 17; cf. v. 1). The suitability of God's timing, though mysterious in nature, provides sufficient warrant for Qoheleth to express hope that judgment will ultimately befall the wicked and vindicate the righteous.

46

Yet, as in 2:13–17, Qoheleth does not dwell on the moral distinctions that profile human character but leaps immediately to acknowledging the fate that befalls *every* living creature, human or otherwise. Just deserts for both heroes and scoundrels pale in comparison with the common fate of all the living. It is unclear, lamentably, what precisely is meant by the sage in verse 18, given the problematic nature of the Hebrew text, except that God somehow has a hand in the common fate of humans and animals. The reference to animals is pejorative; humans are no better than animals, morally or otherwise, which is certainly no complement to the subhuman species! Humanity, thus, deludes itself in thinking that it is a cut above the other living creatures of the earth. A cultured life makes no difference in the end, as Enkidu himself, the man born and raised in the wild, discovered (see Introduction). The wicked are by definition morally deficient, but the righteous too are deficient, given their shared fate with the animals in God's design.

The sage's earnest expectation of judgment between the wicked and the just is apparently defeated by the indiscriminate handling of their respective fates by God. The fate of death undercuts any and all essential distinctions even between human being and beast, despite humanity's regal stature profiled in Genesis 1 and Psalm 8. (Psalm 104, however, makes no qualitative distinction between humans and animals!) In the eyes of the sage, humans and animals share the same breath of life and, hence, return to dust in the same way (cf. Gen. 3:19). Qoheleth can only muster an agnostic position regarding the destiny of the quickening spirit or life-breath (*rûah*) possessed by every living being (cf. Gen. 2:7). The destiny of the life-spirit cannot be ascertained (but cf. Eccl. 12:7). All that is certain is uncertainty.

There remains, however, a more urgent point. The utter uncertainty of life after death highlights in starkest relief the value of the present. The sage commands, once again, the virtues of enjoyment, particularly that of work (3:22), for that is as good as it gets ("there is nothing better") in the face of life's vicissitudes. Enjoyment *in* one's work is one's authentic lot or portion (cf. 2:10). Like an inherited plot of land, such enjoyment must be cultivated, first and foremost by welcoming it in gratitude and then engaging in its immediacy (see 9:10). To strive after unattainable knowledge or to reach for elusive gain is to miss, and thus refuse, the gifts of God. Qoheleth has redefined joy, stripping from it all trappings of gainful pursuit. To appreciate the momentary pleasures of a good meal or a good day's work, one must first come to terms with the global absurdity of human existence—its vanity—in which the future is unknowable, much less controllable. Conversely, grasping what is beyond one's reach is forever "chasing one's tail," to press the animal analogy.

47

Ecclesiastes 4:1–16
The Problem with Power

Having averred the enjoyment of work and conveyed his hope for judgment against the wicked, Qoheleth turns his attention back to those intractable features of human existence that effectively shatter the cause of justice and the meaningfulness of work. His eye ever watchful, the sage does not avert his gaze from the painful realities that invariably frustrate noble ideals and humane concerns, realities hopelessly corrupted by the abuse of power. Throughout this chapter, the sage offers living examples of the all-encompassing scope of vanity.

The Travesties of Toil and Justice (4:1–6)

Without wincing, Qoheleth looks at oppression "under the sun," describing it starkly in terms of the social polarity between the oppressed and the oppressors. What defines this polarity is the possession of power. The inequity of power is the root of all oppression, the sage observes. Hence, it is incumbent upon society to protect the weak from the strong, otherwise the polarizing power of power reigns, leaving no mediating ground within the human community.

Twice Qoheleth laments the lack of comforters among the powerless. By itself, the first mention of "comfort" in verse 1 might convey merely the sense of consolation. Its second occurrence, however, suggests more than simply providing the proverbial tissue to dry the victim's tears. Here, the comforter takes on an active role aimed at protecting the powerless from further abuse by the powerful. The consoler, in short, is an advocate. As the verb "to be comforted" (*nḥm*) can connote repentance or change of mind (e.g., Exod. 32:12–14; Jer. 8:6; 18:10), so its active form as found in Ecclesiastes 4:1 can connote the granting of relief and protection before the lords of power. Such advocacy entails an investment of power in behalf of the powerless, which, Qoheleth laments, no one is willing to grant, certainly not those who possess power. No one is willing to bridge the yawning chasm that separates the powerful from the powerless. As other sages have claimed, crossing the economic gulf begins with the recognition that both the rich and the poor are equal in the eyes of their creator (Prov. 22:2; 29:13). Whereas Israel's visionaries proclaimed God's work to vindicate the poor (Prov. 22:23), to reverse their status (1 Sam. 2:8; Luke 1:52–53), and to enable the meek to inherit the earth (Matt. 5:5), all Qoheleth—the erstwhile or at least incapacitated king—can do is share his tears with those of the oppressed. The irony of Qoheleth's incapacity is unmistakable, for steeped in biblical (and ancient Near East) tradition was the king's mandate to defend the powerless (e.g., Ps. 72:12–14; Prov. 31:8–9). In Ecclesiastes, one finds the death of outrage and the failure of nerve (see 5:8 [Heb. v. 7]).

The apparently hopeless situation of the oppressed leads Qoheleth to consider the advantage of death over life. Death spares the individual from having to witness "all the oppressions under the sun." Living is accursed with the plague of oppression; death is the final comfort, the divester of all power, a realm that levels out all social disparities and inequities of power. Qoheleth pushes his morbid logic to its final conclusion: the best of all possible worlds is the one in which life is never conceived. Yet Qoheleth will later prefer life over death: "[T]here is no work or thought or knowledge or wisdom in Sheol" (9:10; see also 8:15). In that text, the prospect of nonexistence provides the warrant for continued living and working (see 9:4–10). Here, however, death is considered bliss, a desire for which also Jeremiah and Job fervently expressed when they came close to cursing God for their own misery (Job 3:3–26; Jer. 20:14–18).

The thematic movement from oppression (Eccl. 4:1–3) to toil (vv. 4–6) is a natural one, but not as obvious as one might assume. Nowhere does Qoheleth speak of work per se as innately oppressive. The sage does not regard work in itself as a curse, for he does not categorically exclude the possibility of finding enjoyment, and thus meaning, in one's work. Yet Qoheleth does expose the vainglorious abuse of work, which reduces work to toil (see the epilogue of the commentary). While the enterprising application of one's talents and gifts would seem to capture the quintessence of meaningful work, Qoheleth probes deeper and finds that at its root lies an ulterior motive, namely, envy (or "jealousy" [*qin'â*]). More than simply admiration, envy inspires competition and thus twists the noble sense of vocation into an exercise in rivalry, into an upward and onward quest in the pursuit of dominance, leading even to violence. The envy of another (literally "one's neighbor") flies in the face of the great command found in Leviticus and on the lips of Jesus to "love your neighbor as yourself" (Lev. 19:18b; Matt. 22:39). Qoheleth's discovery of envy-inspired toil marks a milestone in his search for the proper motivation that encourages solidarity rather than subjugation in the exercise of toil (see below).

The penetrating sage exposes the danger of any work ethic: work

49

can become all-consuming as a means of gaining supremacy over another. Nowhere does Qoheleth give "healthy competition" the benefit of the doubt. His judgment is uncompromising. As the driving force behind competition in the work place, envy is one form of the demoralizing use of power. And to add insult to injury, the sage points out that the goal of getting ahead of everyone else is a futile pursuit, indeed sheer lunacy ("vanity"), for one's destiny remains unaffected by the amount of toil one exerts.

Again, Qoheleth does not discount work in and of itself, as the following two proverbs attest (Eccl. 4:5–6). Whereas the sage presents the one extreme, namely the *all*-consuming drive to outdo one's neighbor (v. 4), the following proverb conveys the opposite extreme, namely, the *self*-consuming danger of idleness. In classic form, the sage renders a scathing indictment against his favorite foil, the foolish, who are hardly known for their industrious habits (so Prov. 6:6–11; 10:4–5; 12:24; 19:15; 20:13; 24:30–34). "Go to the ant, you lazybones; consider its ways, and be wise," enjoins conventional wisdom (Prov. 6:6). Although "poverty and want" will come "like an armed warrior" (v. 11), fools have only themselves to blame, Qoheleth makes graphically clear (Eccl. 4:5). In idleness, fools consume themselves. As toil can be all-consuming, so idleness is self-cannibalizing. The challenge is to find a balance by gaining a new perspective on the value of work (see 9:7–10 and the epilogue of the commentary).

The following proverb (4:6), a "better-than" saying, nuances the necessity of work espoused in the preceding one. A small amount of quietude or rest is more valuable than a prodigious amount of work, regardless of success. According to ancient Near Eastern myth, the lack of rest and quiet leads only to chaos and tragedy (e.g., *Atrahasis, Enūma eliš*). The value of rest and refreshment also holds a preeminent position in Qoheleth's view (see, e.g., 8:15). If all-consuming work is the bane of human existence, rest constitutes humanity's redemption within the day-to-day routine of living. The sage's insight adds an important anthropological dimension to the theology of sabbath rest (e.g., Gen. 2:1–3; Exod. 20:8–11). Unremitting work is the hallmark of oppression, a dramatic example of which can be found in the story of Israel's experience in Egypt (Exod. 1:13–14). For Qoheleth, an individual's incessant drive to work, even for his or her self-enrichment, is no different from the oppression wielded by a ruthless taskmaster. Power can be wielded against oneself as easily as it can be used against a neighbor or an enemy. Without the benefit of rest, even self-employment is self-enslavement.

Solitude and Solidarity (4:7–12)

The theme of oppressive work spills over into this next section as the value of relationships becomes the focus of the sage's scrutiny. Given his grim outlook on work and life in general, Qoheleth could have easily espoused a form of rugged individualism or survivalism, of "every man for himself" in a dog-eat-dog world. But he does nothing of the sort. Rather, the sage regards as a tragic exemplar of vanity the solitary individual, bereft of family ties (literally, "without sons and brothers") and self-consumed with work. Qoheleth does not have in mind the single, nonmarried person, although he commends spousal relations elsewhere (9:9). The individual whom the sage identifies is one who has renounced all forms of meaningful relationships (cf. Prov. 18:1). Afflicted with an insatiable appetite for wealth, the loner is consumed by work. The statement that the eyes of the toiler are never satisfied with wealth recalls Qoheleth's initial observations in 1:8. As the cosmos lacks any sense of interdependence, each element incessantly locked in its own wearying course, so the insatiable toiler leads a fragmented existence, alone and alienated. That the striving for gain leads to self-deprivation is highlighted all the more in the rhetorical self-questioning that follows: "For whom am I toiling?" It is a question that echoes the plaintive lament of Gilgamesh over losing the secret plant of rejuvenation to the serpent: "For what purpose have my arms grown weary? For what purpose was the blood inside me so red? I did not gain an advantage for myself" (see Introduction). The toiler has only himself or herself to blame.

The question cuts to the heart of the issue. If one's unrelenting toil is in fact for someone else, then one's power and identity are surrendered to another, constituting a form of enslavement. However, the answer in the case of the loner is self-reflexive—"I toil for *myself*"—underscoring all the more the irony of toil. Singularly driven, the loner in Qoheleth's eyes has willfully sacrificed all forms of relationship upon the altar of the ego. Yet this individual is dominated by a taskmaster, albeit of his or her own making. The renunciation of "pleasure" (*ṭôbâ*), which includes the simple joys of sustenance, rest, and relationship, is at base the renunciation of the self in its God-given freedom and capacity for joy. The bankruptcy of toil is due not to any lack of "riches," impermanent that they are, but to the dearth, and consequent death, of joy. And that is bad business. Qoheleth's call is to diversify one's efforts so as to include the reception of joy. The vanity of it all is that unremitting determination and single-minded diligence reap not self-fulfillment but self-deprivation.

In contrast to the loner ("one") are the "two," whose partnership Qoheleth describes in wholly positive terms (vv. 9–11). The point is that only through the other can the individual receive benefit, indeed be saved. The "two," rather than the "one," receive a "good reward for their toil" (v. 9). It is here that Qoheleth comes closest to acknowledging a worthy compensation in the task of toil. Such reward does not entail riches, fame, or glory—all vanity from Qoheleth's perspective. Rather, the bond of solidarity ensures against catastrophe and threat, as well as provides the warmth and affection of companionship necessary for meaningful existence. True security rests not on the exercise of a solitary will but on the ties that bind.

Qoheleth lists three case studies in which companionship proves advantageous. A companion provides rescue, warmth, and a sure defense against physical threat. The middle scenario, which refers to the benefit of "warmth" from another's body, may very well point to a marital relationship (so Targum), but not necessarily, as modern critics are eager to suggest. But if it does have sexual overtones (cf. 1 Kings 1:1–2), the language easily recalls the garden scene of Genesis. There, the LORD GOD observed that "it is not good that the man should be alone" and resolved to create for him a "helper as his partner" (Gen. 2:18–25; cf. Eccl. 4:8). The fact that the woman is created as the man's "counterpartner" (my translation) in work and in fellowship is an evocative testimony of the sustaining power of companionship, which Qoheleth does not deny.

For Qoheleth, the trouble with toil is ultimately resolved in community. The sage finds relationless work, like all-consuming, sabbathless work, to be futile and dehumanizing. It is vanity. Only in community do work and reward find their integral connection. Community, thus, is the "reward" of toil. And in community, one finds true rest and support. Without the bond of companionship, the individual, in addition to being consumed by work, is destined to be helpless during times of crisis and comfortless at all other times (see v. 8). No wonder Qoheleth concludes with a familiar proverb that is attested in similar form in the *Epic of Gilgamesh* (v. 12), a story of two heroic individuals who team up against daunting odds (see Introduction). In this dramatic tale, Enkidu assures his friend Gilgamesh with a proverb of similar sentiment before they face the terrible Humbaba, the formidable guardian of the mythic Cedar Forest.

If two are better than one, three are even better. Or as the French put it more generally, *"l'union fait la force."* Qoheleth, in short, applies a bit of proverbial wisdom—that there is safety in numbers—toward resolving the problematic nature of work. Although the sage derives the value of community and, relatedly, work solely from a pragmatic standpoint, he does point the way to affirming the theological value of community, as crystallized in that proverblike saying of Jesus: "For where two or three are gathered in my name, I am there among them" (Matt. 18:20). Worship too is a matter of work, a "work of the people" (*leitourgia* or liturgy). Community is critical: an individual can no more worship alone than he or she can meaningfully work alone. Worship is by nature collaborative.

Qoheleth's character and quest have undergone a remarkable progression from his self-introduction in 1:12—2:11 to his observations in 4:7–12. In the former passage, Qoheleth introduced himself as king, unsurpassed in stature and deed. Now his observations commend the simple and basic value of collaboration. In the process, Qoheleth has deconstructed all illusions of grandeur, royal and otherwise, and has elevated the import of the ordinary to its most profound level; it is in the mundane that the key to life is to be found. Who, thus, is the tragic "one" in 4:8–12? In Qoheleth's "monumental phase" (2:1–11), the king was the "one," the loner driven and ultimately victimized by his own accomplishments. The sage has deconstructed his identity as king, confirmed all the more by the following passage, in which he returns to the royal ethos with a vengeance.

The "Poverty" of Wisdom (4:13–16)

This final section continues Qoheleth's analysis of the problem of power, specifically economic and political power. The sage notes that wisdom is by no means monopolized by the aged, the powerful, and the rich. Such credentials, which Qoheleth's royal persona clearly possesses, do not necessarily qualify oneself to be wise. To the contrary, poverty and youth—frequently pejorative categories in conventional wisdom—are specifically associated with wisdom by Qoheleth. Indeed, all three categories find their convergence in the form of a narrative vignette about the usurpation of an aging, foolish king by a poor, wise youth. The king's foolishness is defined by his refusal to accept advice. He, too, is a loner by intent. And so by such hardness of mind, the ruler makes himself vulnerable to being replaced by one who is receptive to wise counsel, a mark of wisdom (cf. Prov. 11:14; 15:22). Qoheleth suggests that even a former prisoner from an impoverished background can rise up and replace the king.

Two biblical examples come to mind that dramatically illustrate Qoheleth's point: the rags-to-riches story of Joseph's rise to power in Egypt (Genesis 37—41) and the incident of Rehoboam's disastrous policy that resulted in the secession of the northern tribes (1 Kings 12:1–19). The

53

latter story finds peculiar resonance with Qoheleth's vignette. When Rehoboam refused the advice of his experienced counselors to lighten the "heavy yoke" that Solomon had imposed on the kingdom, a rebellion erupts, led by the fugitive Jeroboam, northern Israel's first king (vv. 6–8). In modern history, comparable examples abound of a former political prisoner or exiled leader not only assuming the country's highest office but replacing an entire regime, for good or ill (e.g., Iran, Nicaragua, South Africa, South Korea). Such is the script of social revolution, whose expressed purpose is to establish a more just or credible rule. It is significant that Qoheleth describes the youthful, wise successor enjoying the widespread support of his subjects. This king is *with* his people, relationally bound to and confirmed by them. As a traditional proverb observes, "The glory of a king is a multitude of people; without people a prince is ruined" (Prov. 14:28).

Yet the young ruler's legacy does not endure. For whatever reason, his successors disparage his reputation. This again proves that one's legacy or remembrance, even established in wisdom, is wasted, subjected to the whims of future generations (cf. 1:11). Today's just governance is tomorrow's forgotten relic. This "historical" anecdote vividly summarizes in parabolic fashion much of what the "royal" sage has espoused earlier: the inefficacy of royal power and accomplishment, the tragedy of the loner, and the lack of an enduring legacy. The "poverty of wisdom," my title for this section, refers to Qoheleth's association of poverty and wisdom as well as to wisdom's ultimate inefficacy in the political realm. This, too, is vanity!

Ecclesiastes 5:1–20
The Simplicity of Reverence

Chapter 5 (Heb. 4:17—5:19) imparts a series of ethically charged observations and advice. Here one also finds a concentration of references to God, indicating the sage's theocentric basis for ethical reflection and conduct. Throughout this passage, Qoheleth urges his readers to lead a life of integrity and simplicity in one's speech and conduct, as an outgrowth of proper reverence for God, the wholly Other.

Simplicity in Speech (5:1–7 [Heb. 4:17—5:6])

Qoheleth stands squarely on the shoulders of his sapiential predecessors when he exhorts a life of simplicity in discourse and conduct.

54

The sage explores the moral contours of appropriate speech and behavior in three forms of discourse that include God in one way or another: sacrifice, prayer, and vows. The sage's opening injunction to "guard your steps" recalls a conventional metaphor in wisdom—the path or way—which can connote righteous or wicked conduct, depending on the direction (e.g., Prov. 1:15–16; 4:27; 5:5; 6:18; 19:2).

Qoheleth opens his moral exhortations with the particular setting of the temple. Within its sacred precincts, listening is deemed more appropriate than sacrifice, particularly sacrifice offered by fools. The efficacy of sacrifice depends entirely upon the character of the presenter; hence, offerings made by those who cannot refrain from committing evil—or who are unable to recognize that they are committing evil—are worthless, even self-condemning. Indeed, it is from such a perspective that Malachi indicts the temple priesthood (Mal. 1:10). Psalm 50, too, exposes the inadequacy of sacrifice from God's perspective, since "the world and all that is in it is mine" (Ps. 50:12b). God, thus, has no "physical" need for slaughtered animals. Consequently, the psalmist commends only those sacrifices that are offered in thanksgiving and the payment of vows (v. 14), activities also enjoined, not coincidentally, by Qoheleth (Eccl. 5:4–5 [Heb. vv. 3–4]). More broadly, the preference for right conduct over sacrifice is attested frequently in biblical tradition (e.g., 1 Sam. 15:22: Prov. 21:3; Isa. 1:12–17; Hos. 6:6; Amos 5:21–24; Micah 6:6–8).

Qoheleth's foremost concern, however, is for speech. Within the sacred precincts, silence is in order. Listening to God indicates obedience (*šm'*). The sage's exhortation may very well draw from an ancient cultic ethos that Yehezkel Kaufmann and more recently Israel Knohl have referred to as "the sanctuary of silence" (Knohl, pp. 17–30). Within the sanctuary, while sacrifices were conducted, silence reigned, fostering a sense of divine presence and human receptivity. Similarly, Rudolph Otto stresses the importance of liturgical silence as a way of encountering the holy: such silence is "no mere momentary pause, but an absolute cessation of sound long enough to 'hear the silence' itself" (Otto, p. 70). Such "sheer silence" characterized Elijah's encounter with God (1 Kings 19:12). In consort with priestly tradition, Qoheleth urges an economizing of speech in the sacral setting and, more generally, as a part of life. The ever-present temptation of rash speech is made all the more dangerous in worship in that one becomes unwittingly trapped into promising things that he or she cannot keep or finds inconvenient (cf. Lev. 5:4).

Such self-entanglement only provokes God's anger (Eccl. 5:6), since indiscriminately conveying one's thoughts and petitions to God only trivializes the Deity (v. 2). God becomes merely a tool of human

55

manipulation, subject to the petitioner's every desire. Moreover, God is demeaned when one procrastinates in fulfilling his or her vow (see also Deut. 23:21 [Heb. v. 22]). Qoheleth urges discretion in discourse and urgency in deed for fulfilling what has been promised, particularly before God or the priest ("messenger" in Eccl. 4:6). Indeed, Qoheleth suggests that it is better not to swear at all (5:5 [Heb. v. 4]). The sage's words are in fact echoed by Jesus in the Sermon on the Mount: "Do not swear at all, either by heaven, for it is the throne of God, or by the earth, for it is his footstool. . . . Let your word be 'Yes, Yes' or 'No, No'; anything more than this comes from the evil one" (Matt. 5:34–35, 37). Simplicity in speech is key, for it reflects the integrity of the speaker and genuine reverence for God (see Matt. 6:7–8).

Like Jesus, Qoheleth offers a terse theological rationale for guarding one's speech: "God is in heaven, and you upon earth; therefore let your words be few" (Eccl. 5:2 [Heb. v. 1]; cf. Matt. 5:34). Perhaps more forcefully developed than most sages, Qoheleth's theology avers that God is beyond human heart and mind, beyond human feelings and thoughts, beyond human expectations and desires. Directly tied to the sage's theocentric view are his ethical prescriptions. One cannot strip the surrounding admonitions from their theological center given in Ecclesiastes 5:2 (Heb. v. 1). An awareness of divine transcendence sustains an economy of human discourse, Qoheleth claims. If God were utterly immanent, residing wholly within one's heart, as some today might claim, then free license would be given for human discourse and imagination to run rampant, so Qoheleth's logic would suggest. But the mouth is both a source of sin and an instrument of truth and healing, the sage notes in accordance with sapiential tradition (e.g., Prov. 10:19, 21; 15:1; 18:4, 6, 20; cf. Mark 7:14–15). While the thoughtful word is edifying, rash words quickly destroy and cause irreparable harm. God is not in one's heart any more than God is lodged in a person's mouth. For Qoheleth, divine immanence alone fosters only human contrivance. The Almighty is not party to anyone's secret desires or machinations. "God is in heaven," and the gulf that separates the creature from the Creator mandates spareness of speech that reflects integrity and proper reverence.

As wholly Other, God holds people accountable for what they say and do. God's transcendence is far from connoting divine indifference to human conduct and petition (contra Longman, p. 151). To the contrary, human intransigence and indifference can provoke God's anger (5:6). For Qoheleth, divine distance is in fact charged with ethical significance. God's transcendence counters the vain tendency to proliferate "weasel words," words by which human beings cleverly shirk their moral responsibility or leave room for manipulating the Deity in consonance with their own selfish goals. Human beings can no more change the course of the divine will (see 3:14) as they can transcend their lot in life, Qoheleth claims. As lasting gain is ruled out in Qoheleth's anthropology, so manipulation of the Deity is excluded from his theology.

The proliferation of speech is just one more sign of humanity's tendency to inflate itself and rise above binding obligations, whether self-declared (e.g., "vow") or divinely imposed (e.g., "commandment"), and thereby attempt to breach the boundary of heaven. In the incessant blather of fools, the attempt is made to rebuild the Tower of Babel, and now only with words! Yet, as in the land of Shinar, such an edifice will always remain in ruins (see Gen. 11:1–10). "Why should God be angry at your words and destroy the work of your hands?" Qoheleth asks (Eccl. 5:6). The pretense behind the babble is countered by Qoheleth's call to authentic reverence. Deity and duty, divine transcendence and human integrity, are inseparably intertwined in Qoheleth's moral vision, for "God is in heaven, and you upon earth; therefore let your words be few."

The preference for prolixity is also associated with dreams. Qoheleth may have the ancient practice of incubation in mind, a form of nocturnal divination, or, more broadly, the countless visions purportedly received by seers, prophets, and apocalypticists from which whole books have been fashioned (e.g., Deut. 13:1–5; Isa. 29:7; Dan. 2:1; 7:1; Joel 2:28; Zech. 1:8; 4:1). In any case, the sage questions the significance of dreams. For every dream there is a multitude of interpretations, as any psychologist can attest. As meaningless blather characterizes the fool's discourse, so dreams can be accompanied by much needless preoccupation. Yet it is all for naught: dreams are nothing more than the unchecked imaginings of the unconscious. Consequently, nothing good can come from them any more than wisdom can be culled from the nonsense of fools. Although dreams may seem terrifyingly or alluringly real, they are wholly vacuous fabrications, according to the sage who has seen everything. They are "vanities," no more useful than senseless speech (5:3, 7a [Heb. vv. 2, 6a]). Like prophetic utterances of the future, dreams may suggest that something new is at hand (cf. 1:10). But as the sage has repeatedly stated, "There is nothing new under the sun." Divine reverence or "fear of God" (5:7b [Heb. v. 6b]), by contrast, is entirely real and eminently edifying, for it constitutes the compulsive, moral force behind the fulfillment of duty and the driving rationale behind discriminating, thoughtful speech.

Where the Buck Stops (5:8–9 [Heb. vv. 7–8])

This difficult passage begins with a straightforward observation regarding rampant injustice, a prominent theme in Ecclesiastes (cf.

3:16–17; 4:1–3). Here, most explicitly, is the sage's observation of *economic* disparity in the land. There is no silver lining in his assessment: the "oppression of the poor" is equated with the "violation of justice and right" (5:8 [Heb. v. 7]). The association of justice with righteousness cuts across prophetic, sapiential, and royal rhetoric in the Bible. The ancient Near Eastern king was commonly expected to uphold justice and righteousness in order to ensure the blessings of the land and the integrity of his kingdom (e.g., 2 Sam. 8:15; 1 Kings 10:9; Ps. 72:2). For the prophets, the establishment of justice and righteousness constituted the moral baseline for every reign, current and future (e.g., Isa. 9:7 [Heb. v. 6]; 16:5; Jer. 22:3, 15; Ezek. 45:9; cf. Prov. 31:8–9). Qoheleth notes that "in a province" of his day, the very foundation of kingship and community has been effectively overturned. But this is no surprise, as it was nothing new for the prophets of old.

Uniquely perplexing, perhaps, is Qoheleth's counsel against being overly concerned with or even surprised about rampant injustice. Violations of justice are seemingly routine at any level of human governance. They are part and parcel of a socially stratified existence sustained by bureaucratic indifference and complicity. One official watches over another, and one higher up watches the first ad infinitum. Qoheleth may be claiming that if there were any avenue of appeal or advocacy on behalf of the poor, it would simply dissipate in a bureaucratic quagmire, as some interpreters have suggested. But the sage's assessment reflects a more sinister aspect, as indicated in the term for "high official" (*gābōah*), a unique term for denoting a bureaucrat. Indeed, the term literally means high or haughty one. As Seow points out, it can refer to any arrogant individual who is climbing the economic ladder of success at the expense of the poor (Seow, *Ecclesiastes*, pp. 203–4). The following verse suggests, however, a stratified arrangement of power specifically within the administrative ranks. Someone watching over or guarding (*šmr*) someone else implies a hierarchy of differentiated power, one that reflects not so much a structure of checks-and-balances as a network of corruption in which royal personnel, driven by pride and ambition, ensure their mutual advantage over the dispossessed, a sanctioned conspiracy of corruption. Such "violation of justice" is conducted with impunity. More than bureaucratic indifference, sanctioned extortion seems to be at the heart of the local administration, a corruption by consent.

The extent of corruption does not stop with the local authorities, however, but reaches ineluctably to the top, the king (v. 9). Textually, this verse is a *crux interpretum;* its meaning is unclear, more so in the Hebrew. The mention of land and its gain in this passage suggests that

58

the land's yield is the fundamental issue of contention among unjust bureaucrats and the poor. Indeed, for ancient Israel, whether in the eighth or the fourth century, the equitable use and protection of the land was the foundation of justice. As James L. Mays rightly points out,

> The land was not only the basic economic good in society, essential to well-being, but it also bestowed identity; it was the instrument of participation in the society as an equal, the foundation of freedom. . . . A share in ownership of the basic economic good was a corollary to membership in the society. A free participation in economic power by all citizens was to be maintained and protected. For the ownership of land to become the basis of power for one citizen over another was a perversion of its purpose. (Mays, p. 11)

Simply put, the poor are by definition dispossessed of arable land, whereas the rich are those "who join house to house, who add field to field" (Isa. 5:8). But such amassment of land among the rich brings no advantage to either the land or the community. The "advantage for a land" lies simply in its cultivation as a "plowed field," not in its being part of the king's extensive property. "A king for a plowed field" is Qoheleth's severe qualification of royal might, power that can be easily wielded at the land's expense. The syntax of the sage's elliptical remark may conjure up for the modern reader King Richard III's desperate cry at the conclusion of Shakespeare's brutal tragedy, "A horse! a horse! my kingdom *for* a horse!" But is the royal sage willing to give away the kingdom simply for a cultivated field? More likely, Qoheleth is echoing the sentiment found in Prov. 29:4:

> By justice a king gives stability to the land,
> but one who makes heavy exactions ruins it.

The proverbial sage is quick to commend the kind of king who is beneficial to the "land," namely, one who executes justice. Any rule less than just will only ruin the land. Qoheleth, similarly, is convinced that the kingdom of his day is anything but salutary for the land's sake (cf. Eccl. 10:16–17). Justice in the land is not a luxury of royal policy, but its very basis. In other words, "a king [exists] for [the sake of] a plowed field."

Human history and culture began in a cultivated garden, not within a royal palace or city, the Yahwist of Genesis claims. According to Isaiah, righteousness emerges from the ground up, miraculously germinating from the cultivated wasteland and "abid[ing] in the fruitful field" (Isa. 32:16; 45:8). For Qoheleth, the king and all his administration are there to serve the land and cultivate justice. But a king who "loves the soil" is hard to find (2 Chron. 26:10). Along with the

59

Yahwist of the Pentateuch, the sage is fully cognizant of the abuse of royal power upon the poor and the community as a whole. Yet all he can do is lament, wishing for a king who can recultivate the land with equity. Such a king is not Qoheleth.

The Trouble with Wealth (5:10–17 [Heb. vv. 9–16])

In this section, Qoheleth details the problematic nature of hoarding wealth. Like the insatiable eye and ear (1:8), the one who relentlessly seeks a profit is never satisfied (5:10 [Heb. v. 9]); human voracity is limitless. The vanity of consumption lies in the realization that money never delivers what the earner expects from it. As king, Qoheleth expected his wealth and accomplishments to ensure an enduring remembrance, lasting fame and reputation, the next best thing to immortality (2:1–11, 12–17). But in the consumption of wealth, the consumer, although "increased" economically—not to mention physically!—gains nothing in the end. The reference to eating in 5:11 (Heb. v. 10) is fraught with metaphorical meaning that is economic in background. Qoheleth concedes that human beings are by nature economic beings; hence, all people are in varying degrees consumers. There are those who are on the top of the "food chain," as it were, and there are those who are on the bottom. The distance between them is infinite, and Qoheleth tells his readers what life at the top looks like from down under: like acquisition for its own sake, like obtainment as its own reward. Like greed.

Other than registering disgust and resignation, Qoheleth does not struggle with rectifying the systemic problem of economic disparity. The sage, admittedly, is no revolutionary. Yet he is far from endorsing the status quo and particularly the lifestyles of the rich and famous. To the contrary, Qoheleth sees little gain from such hyperconsumption. The only benefit he concedes in amassing possessions is the opportunity to "see them" (5:11 [Heb. v. 10]), a simple, unglorious fact that bears profound implications. Although many goods can be possessed by persons of means, they remain distant, apprehensible only by sight and, consequently, inefficacious, unable to deliver what the owner expects of them. The possessor cannot truly appropriate possessions to the extent that they enable him or her to be fully satisfied. Possessing something cannot ensure that one will live longer, gain incontestable power, or appropriate life in all its joyous possibilities. Consumption, in short, does not render contentment; it simply leads to more consumption, a vicious cycle. Qoheleth observes that the rich never reach that level of sufficiency in which amassing more becomes irrelevant. Like streams flowing into the bottomless sea (cf. 1:7), wealth does not fulfill, and therein lies the vanity.

In contrast to the self-obsession of the rich, "sweet is the sleep of laborers" (5:12 [Heb. v. 11]), a poignantly telling statement coming from one who presented himself as a king on par with Solomon's legendary status. A comparison is made between the bliss of rest and the overindulgence of the rich. The laborers or servants are able to rest and be refreshed, regardless of the amount they consume. The rich, however, are incessantly preoccupied with pushing the limits of consumption; to them the sky is the limit. Consumption is a curse that afflicts even one's sleep (see also 2:23).

To underscore the trouble with wealth, Qoheleth presents a parable of sorts, an exemplary vignette that serves as an object lesson (5:13–14 [Heb. vv. 12–13]). It illustrates a worst-case scenario ("a grievous ill") in which hoarded wealth was suddenly lost in a bad investment, leaving the erstwhile rich (literally "rich man") empty-handed with nothing to give to their progeny ("son"). The example highlights a paradox: riches "kept" are riches lost. Qoheleth is not claiming that all investments are bad and therefore one should hide his or her possessions out of fear (cf. 11:2 and the parable of the talents in Matt. 25:14–30). Rather, the sage affirms that associating ultimate significance with the proliferation and consumption of wealth is itself a bad venture. Indeed, the desire for wealth is injurious not only to oneself but also to one's family. Whereas Qoheleth complains elsewhere about his lack of control in determining who would inherit or receive his wealth (e.g., 2:18–21; 6:1–2), he laments here of the possibility of having nothing at all to pass on!

This tragic vignette exemplifies a larger claim that can be summed up, albeit banally, with the adage, "You can't take it with you." Qoheleth's point is in line with Jesus' parable of the rich fool in Luke 12:13–21, which dramatically illustrates that "one's life does not consist in the abundance of possessions" (v. 15). Human existence is marked by "naked come, naked go" (cf. Eccl. 1:4; 3:20), an awareness that Job also expresses (Job 1:21; cf. Sir. 40:1; 1 Tim. 6:7). If not from life's vicissitudes, then by death, riches gained are invariably lost. The attempt to secure permanent gain is nothing but "toiling for the wind," a vain exercise. In Ecclesiastes 5:17 [Heb. v. 16], death casts a long shadow over the sage's discussion on wealth: Qoheleth consistently associates "darkness" with either death or misery (e.g., 2:14; 6:4; 12:2). The overly consumptive rich, in effect, live in virtual death, wracked by resentment while all the time consuming themselves. Their fate is no different from that of fools, who through their idleness consume their own flesh (4:6;

61

cf. 2:14)! The irony is complete: whether through hopeless indolence or excessive industry, the tragedy of an unfulfilled or discontented life is the inevitable result. The opposite of contentment, "resentment," is the privilege, as it were, of the self-obsessed rich, a self-directed wrath resulting from a life that has sought to gain the world and, in turn, has grasped only air. Yet, Qoheleth contends, while death trumps every achievement and plan, there is still room for joy in the hospice called life "under the sun." The affliction of the rich, coined "affluenza" in modern parlance, is symptomatic of the search for sufficiency in all the wrong places. Rich in money are the wealthy, but dead broke in all the ways that matter.

Preoccupied with Joy (5:18–20 [Heb. vv. 17–19])

Of all the vain and tragic dimensions of human existence, there is also something "good" under the sun, namely the three gifts of joy, a trinity of delight: eating, drinking, and enjoying one's work. This section marks the antithesis to the preceding section. Over and against a life fraught with resentment (5:13–17 [Heb. vv. 12–16]), Qoheleth offers a way toward contentment. Unlike the obsessive quest for gain described above, the simple pleasures of sustenance and work somehow find their salutary mark within an individual's tragically limited life. Whereas death deconstructs all sense of ultimate gain and gratification, it also sets in stark relief the redemptive import of these simple gifts.

The paradox is tersely presented at the conclusion of verse 18. The theme of death is more prominent here than in the sage's previous commendations of enjoyment (cf. 1:24–26; 2:3b; 3:12–13, 22). Enjoyment for the sage is a deadly serious matter. The shortness of an individual's existence ("the few days of life") serves not to neutralize but rather to underscore, all the more, the efficacy of life's simple pleasures. Death for Qoheleth does not *temper*, much less deconstruct, the joyous dimensions of life, as some interpreters tend to read the sage's commendations. Like darkness enhancing the weak radiance of a candle, death serves to *highlight*, rather than extinguish, those all-too-fleeting moments of joy. While death devalues life defined exclusively in terms of gain and self-enrichment, it nevertheless heightens the value of these simple gifts.

Such is the mixed lot of mortals, which embraces both the delight and the drudgery, the joy amid life's brevity. One portion of that "lot" (*ḥēleq*) is like a plot of fertile land, passed on from one generation to the next. It is the apportioned "field of dreams," of joyous episodes and moments that constitute an integral part of the limited and rugged landscape of human existence. On the one hand, to *demand* that lot, as in the case of the prodigal son (Luke 15:12), and to try to wrest from it the means of self-glory and escape from responsibility is to violate its integrity as God's gift. This portion of joy is distorted into something to be grasped and hoarded, a product of obsessive toiling, yet never fulfilling a person's self-obsessed expectations. On the other hand, this inheritance requires cultivation, specifically a cultivated awareness, so that its yield is developed and savored as a source of delight and respite.

Qoheleth includes without fail in his commendations the matter of finding enjoyment *in* one's toil. Work is not denounced but in fact encouraged (cf. 9:10). Consequently, the simple pleasures of life are by no means an exit from oppressive toil but, rather, part of the necessary rhythm of work, rest, and sustenance. More than simply antidotes for the tragic frailty of human existence, more than providing psychological relief, these simple pleasures are in a fundamental sense redemptive. The "lot" to which Qoheleth refers is a *given*. It requires work and provides enjoyment, but it is never the object of pursuit or one's grasping (see also 2:21). The person who welcomes his or her lot in life is like a farmer who cultivates the land as a way of life in his love affair with the soil, yet whose yield is fully dependent upon the rain from heaven.

The redemptive nature of these moments of joy lies first and foremost in the recognition that they are gifts from God. Indeed, the ability to enjoy simple pleasures is itself a divinely inspired capacity (cf. 6:2). Wealth, consequently, is not necessarily the mark of a compulsive, vain lifestyle; it, too, can be received as a gift rather than grasped as a means for self-apotheosis. Wealth is devalued when it is employed as a means; its luster shines brightly, however, when it is enjoyed in gratitude for its own sake and—to push Qoheleth's thought a bit further— shared. (Relationships marked by sharing and mutual support are, in fact, highly valued by Qoheleth [4:9–12; 11:1]). Furthermore, the ability to enjoy such gifts prevents one from "brooding," literally "calling to mind" (*zkr;* 5:20 [Heb. v. 19]). Such brooding suggests a wallowing in nostalgia and, perhaps, a desperate longing for some sweet hereafter. In either case, there is a denial or discounting of the blessings of the present. "Nostalgia" denotes the painful (*-algia*) return home (*nostos*). Such pain is marked by a denial of the present and a disillusionment with the limited and seemingly insignificant span of one's life ("all the days of one's life" v. 20 [Heb. v. 19]; cf. v. 18 [Heb. v. 17]). Resentment is its cause (v. 17 [Heb. v. 16]).

63

Ecclesiastes 6:1–12
The Limits of Desire

As chapter 5 concludes with the gift of enjoyment, so chapter 6 treats the obsession that kills enjoyment. The following collection of sayings illustrates joy's polar opposite, desire.

The Inability to Enjoy (6:1–6)

True to his comprehensive analysis of human existence, Qoheleth views both the "good" and the "grievous." Having delineated the good, the sage returns to describe an "evil" with which humankind is burdened. He introduces the case of an individual who has received from God an abundance of wealth, yet cannot enjoy it. This example constitutes an arbitrary reversal of what is described in 5:18 (Heb. v. 17), in which Qoheleth claims wealth and its enjoyment as gifts of God. As primary agent, God gives and withholds; God is both the giver of material blessings and the withholder of the opportunity to enjoy (literally, "consume") such blessings. The inability to enjoy, however, stems not from some psychological fault of the person who has received such abundance but, rather, from a larger, social predicament: a "stranger," rather than the original recipient/owner, is given the opportunity to enjoy God's gifts. The precise identity of this "stranger" is cloaked in mystery. Qoheleth had earlier complained of having to leave the products of his toil to "those who come after me," "master[s] of all for which I toiled and used my wisdom under the sun" (2:18b–19). This "stranger" is the one "who did not toil for it" (v. 21). This enigmatic figure is both the undeserving recipient of another person's earnings profiled in 2:18–21 and now the threatening outsider depicted in 6:2.

The figure of the "stranger" or "outsider" looms large in the worldview of the biblical wisdom traditions. In Proverbs, the archetypal stranger is wisdom's nemesis, identical in gender but wholly opposite in character (Prov. 2:16; 5:3; 6:24; 7:4–5). Woman stranger is the personified threat to the family; she is a covenant breaker and seducer, a veritable anti-*sophia* (wisdom), whereas wisdom's mission is to uphold the community in its integrity. The conflict embodied by these two mythic characters in Proverbs 1—9 reflects a pattern of social conflict in postexilic Israel. During this period, Palestine was filled with both indigenous and immigrant populations, the "people of the land" and the returning exiles or *gōlâ* (see, e.g., Ezra 3:3; 4:1; 6:16; 9:1–2; Neh. 9:24, 30; 10:30–31). It was a time when land and family were issues of great contention. Consequently, one's family roots played a decisive role in reclaiming land that was once lost in exile, not unlike the situation in Palestine today.

Who are the rightful heirs? Who are the intruders? These questions can be answered in various ways, depending upon one's perspective. In any case, the author of Ecclesiastes, living also during this tumultuous time, complains of the threat posed by the stranger who receives what someone else has earned. By divine default, as it were, one is continually at risk of losing his or her possessions to someone else, someone outside one's familial sphere. Possessions are held firmly in the owner's hand only to slip through his or her fingers and be caught by the stranger, who by definition has no right or familial claim to them. Ownership is, thus, a misnomer. One's possessions are exclusively gifts of God, and as easily as God gives, so God takes away to give to others. The givenness of material possessions is a two-edged sword.

The sage follows his example with the hypothetical illustration (cf. 5:13–15 [Heb. vv. 12–14]) of a patriarch who sired a hundred children and lived "a thousand years twice over," but for whatever reason could not enjoy "life's good things" or receive a proper burial (site?). Qoheleth counters the widespread sentiment that a large family is eminently preferable (cf. Ps. 127:4). Job had only a tenth of the number of children of Qoheleth's patriarch (Job 1:2)! The reference to the man's lack of a burial (site), although appearing abrupt in context, indicates the poignant irony of having a large family but without the expected benefits. On the one hand, the unwillingness of children to give their parent a proper burial is nothing less than a travesty of justice. On the other hand, the quest to secure or prearrange one's burial site could be considered a mark of arrogance (Isa. 22:15–16).

In any case, Qoheleth concludes that it is better to have been a stillborn child (cf. 4:3). There are the living who enter and leave the domain of life naked and empty-handed (5:15 [Heb. v. 14]), and there is the stillborn who enters vanity and darkness (6:4). "Vanity" here connotes the reality of life dispelled, of a life never lived outside the womb, a name and identity never unveiled, the tragedy of tragedies. Yet the sage boldly claims that such a fate is preferable to a life that has exceeded Methuselah's span more than two-fold (Gen. 5:26–27)! What makes nonexistence preferable to two thousand years of living is simple: the former has achieved rest. A long life without enjoyment (literally "seeing good" [Eccl. 6:6]) is far worse than no life at all. The

65

stillborn is spared the misery of consciousness (v. 5). Qoheleth here acknowledges that cognition is inextricably linked to vexation, and lack of consciousness is tantamount to relief and rest (cf. 1:18). But in either case, the end is the same, namely, the bliss of death. Death, once again, trumps the kind of life that seeks to immortalize itself in reputation. Such a life, however, leads only to frustration and resentment. The key to life, as the sage has intimated earlier, is found in the ability to enjoy the temporary, relative goods, given by God, on their own terms.

Sight, Appetite, and the Impotency of Wisdom (6:7–9)

Insatiable craving afflicts the human condition, Qoheleth claims. Although all labor is for the mouth, the gullet, like the sea, never fills up (1:7), or like the eyes, it is never satisfied (1:8; 4:8). Indeed, the appetite can be compared to death itself, which is indiscriminate and insatiable (cf. Prov. 27:20; 30:15–16). The result or gain of work, thus, cannot be the foundation for happiness, the sage contends, for it does not satisfy any more than hoarding possessions or cultivating fleeting fame can. The inefficacy of work leads directly to the question of character: the wise, who are known by their high work ethic, have no ultimate advantage over the foolish, who are anything but industrious (see Eccl. 4:5). And then there are the poor who are discerning and prudent (literally "know how to walk before the living") yet remain poor (6:8b). Elsewhere, Qoheleth takes pains to show that the rich do not hold a monopoly on wisdom (4:13; 9:15). But "what do the poor have?" the sage asks rhetorically. If the wise have no advantage over the foolish, what can wisdom offer the poor to help them overcome their economic misery? Wisdom proves itself powerless.

The inefficacy of toil leads directly to the impotency of wisdom. Yet Qoheleth makes a commendation in verse 9: the sight of the eyes is preferable to the "wandering of desire" (literally, the "going of the gullet"). "Seeing good" is one of Qoheleth's formulae for enjoyment and, thus, for living (e.g., 2:1; 3:13; 5:11, 18 [Heb. vv. 10, 17]; cf. 3:22). Here, Qoheleth takes a significant step toward defining his vision of the good life by making a crucial distinction between "seeing good," on the one hand, and "devouring good," on the other. Earlier, the sage had asked what gain there was in owning goods except "to see them" (5:11 [Heb. v. 10]). Enjoyment is not a matter of desire. The problem with rampant consumption is its insatiable appetite, which results in only discontent and resentment (6:2). Although the eyes discern and appreciate the good, they do not devour it like the mouth and gullet as the means for self-aggrandizement. While sight can appreciate the gift as gift, desire, like a craving appetite, tragically attempts to consume it. Joy is received,

66

even partaken, as in the simple gifts of food and drink, but it cannot be consumed as the object of desire. In the consumptive *pursuit* of happiness, joy will prove as elusive as chasing the wind.

Here, as elsewhere, Qoheleth points out the limitation of appropriating the good. This is a "vanity," the leitmotif of Qoheleth's protestation against the confining limitations of life. Inasmuch as it is impossible to capture the wind bare-handed, it is imprudent, indeed self-destructive, to direct one's life toward the singular goal of consuming what is neither attainable nor efficacious. To *see* the good must suffice, and to be content with the sufficiency of seeing is itself a gift. Although Qoheleth mentions eating and drinking as an integral part of enjoyment (e.g., 3:22), the sage takes a radically minimalistic stance compared with the all-consuming quest for wealth and power by those, including Qoheleth once, who cannot get enough (2:1–11). Qoheleth's joy, in short, is not a feast but a fast.

Who Knows the Good? (6:10–12)

This transitional section comprises a series of questions, the first verse of which marks the physical midpoint of the book, according to the Masoretes who made notation of this in the margin. Although the Hebrew is difficult, the verse recalls 1:9–10, which denies the existence of novelty in the course of human history (see also 3:15). Here, similar language is employed to assert a form of predestination. Whatever happens has been destined; identity and destiny are bound up together by name. The world of the "already named" is comprehensively cosmic and human. As for human beings (*'ādām*), their destiny is sealed.

Most commentators find this clause of verse 10b abrupt, if not meaningless, in its immediate context and frequently resort to various emendations (see Seow, *Ecclesiastes,* p. 231). The contextual connection, however, is blatantly obvious: the "name" referred to in the previous clause is applied to *'ādām,* the human agent of what is done under the sun. The name *'ādām,* in fact, reveals both an identity and a destiny in another prominent biblical tradition, namely Gen. 2:4b—3:24. Primal man is formed "from the dust of the ground," *'ādām* from the *'ădāmâ* ("ground"). Humanity is, thus, a "groundling," finite and frail, whose genesis and destiny are equivalent: "You [will] return to the ground, for out of it you were taken; you are dust, and to dust you shall return" (Gen. 3:19). Qoheleth observes a similar equivalency of genesis and destiny: "All are dust, and all turn to dust again" (Eccl. 3:20); "As they came from their mother's womb, so they shall go again, naked as they came" (5:15a [Heb. v. 14a]). The images of dust and frailty, inextricably linked to the

67

image of humanity, serves to underscore humanity's finitude, destined by God. Humanity is bound to limitation; it cannot request a name change.

Although not mentioned by name in the series of passive constructions in 6:10, God, the determiner of names, is the implied subject. God is, moreover, the "stronger" one (the NRSV misleadingly pluralizes the Hebrew), and disputing (*dîn*) with God is futile. Only here does Qoheleth come close to Job. Job complains of God's overpowering strength, which undercuts divine justice (e.g., Job 9:1–12). No one can say to God, "What are you doing?" (cf. Eccl. 8:4) and thereby call the Almighty to account, even if all evidence points to a miscarriage of justice, Job complains (Job 9:12). Yet such a realization of God's incontestable strength does not prevent Job from vociferously pressing God to appear in court for questioning (9:32–35; 16:18–22). In fact, God does appear before Job to answer his accusations (38—41). For Qoheleth, however, there is no contending, and therefore no resolving, with the Almighty. Qoheleth is never granted divine solution to the vanities of life; he is not privy to special revelation. The sage remains on earth as God resides in heaven (Eccl. 5:2 [Heb. v. 1]).

Before God's unmatchable transcendence, human discourse finds its limitations (5:2b; 6:11). "Let your words be few," Qoheleth advises in 5:2 (Heb. v. 1). In 6:11, he observes a proportionate increase of "vanity" in tandem with the proliferation of words. Words lose their efficacy before the one who is stronger, yet there are those who babble on ad nauseum, hopelessly deluded that something will change, or that God will be more favorably inclined to their desires as a result. Qoheleth's limiting view of language, it should be noted, runs counter to much biblical tradition, which stresses the efficacy of the word directed to, or imparted by, God. From Moses and Habakkuk to Job and the psalmist, urgent petitions and complaints are registered throughout the biblical corpus to elicit nothing less than a change of heart in God (cf. Exod. 32:11–14; Hab. 2:1–2; Jon. 3:9–10; Pss. 44; 89). Qoheleth, however, will have none of that. God's ways are inscrutable; all that is certain is the unassailable strength and unwavering resolve of the Deity. God accomplishes what God wills. All petition is futile.

Striking at the heart of performative speech, Qoheleth's criticism of human discourse is nothing less than radical. According to biblical tradition, the utterance of a word, whether prophetic, petitionary, or sapiential, unleashes a force with which to be reckoned. Performative words are considered world-creating words; they embody a formative, causal power either for woe or for weal. "Death and life are in the power of the tongue, and those who love it will eat its fruits," notes one anonymous sage (Prov. 18:21). "Those who despise the word bring destruc-

68

tion on themselves," warns another (13:13a). Speech can be edifying or destructive (12:6; 16:27; 18:6). Qoheleth's indictment, however, seems to undermine all esteem over the spoken word. Whatever is "created" by the utterance of a word, whether it is a world of praise or a setting of judgment, is simply a house of cards, ready to crumble at the slightest breath of God. It is "vanity." Rather than building up or tearing down (cf. Jer. 1:9–10), the proclaimed word establishes not settings of sustenance and conviction, of hope and transformation, but only mirages, empty and desolate. The famous speech of the narrator in Flaubert's *Madame Bovary* poignantly captures the limitations of speech: "[H]uman speech is like a cracked kettle on which we strum out tunes to make a bear dance, when we would move the stars to pity" (quoted from Brink, p. 129).

Yet Qoheleth is not out to deconstruct language entirely; he himself is a master of words. Although verbosity is not Qoheleth's literary trademark, his indictment against prolixity in verse 11 is conveyed with the poetic elegance of classic Hebraic form, compact and alliterative (but cf. 1:6, 11). The sage's words, an epilogist claims, are like "goads" (12:11). Sharp and pointed, they serve to burst the bubbles of human presumption. That words, spoken and read, constitute the essential material for teaching Qoheleth does not deny. What the sage seeks is a new integrity for human discourse, one anticipated by his sagacious predecessors who frequently exhorted restraint and rigor in the deployment of discourse (e.g., Prov. 10:11, 19; 12:18; 15:1, 4, 23). Implicit is Qoheleth's particular distaste for words used in self-inflating ways. "So how is one the better?" asks Qoheleth. What edification is to be gained from profuse and banal speech? Human words, like dreams (cf. Eccl. 5:3, 7 [Heb. vv. 2, 6]), bear the danger of creating false worlds, which may seem tangibly real and tempting but ultimately prove vacuous and bogus. Illusions of grandeur typically lie behind such cacophony.

Mark Twain, in his inimitable way, recounts an official communication from the "Office of the Recording Angel" to a certain Abner Scofield regarding his innumerable requests:

> I must once more remind you that we grant no Sunday School Prayers of Professional Christians of the classification technically known in this office as the John Wanamaker grade. We merely enter them as "words.". . . Your remaining 401 details count for wind only. We bunch them and use them for head winds in retarding the ships of improper people, but it takes so many of them that we cannot allow anything for their use. (Twain, pp. 120–21)

Windy words have no use, both Twain and Qoheleth are in firm agreement. For preachers in particular, the swollen and self-reflective use of

69

speech in the pulpit may be symptomatic of something even more acute. Pearl S. Buck humorously recounts the time her father, Absalom Sydenstricker, was a missionary in China. In one city, his lengthy sermon began to make the congregation get restless, causing some members to walk out. Buck writes:

> My father was disturbed, however, and a kindly old lady on the front seat, seeing this, was moved to turn her head and address the people thus: "Do not offend this good foreigner! He is making a pilgrimage in our country so that he may acquire merit in heaven. Let us help him to save his soul!" (Buck, p. 199)

Some preachers preach as if they were trying to save their *own* soul!

Qoheleth's caveat on human speech presents a direct challenge to communities of faith today. Augustine suggested that a person "speaks more or less wisely to the extent that he [or she] has become more or less proficient in the Holy Scriptures" (Augustine, p. 122). Poet and writer Kathleen Norris draws from Augustine's criterion by noting that the church today has failed to cultivate what she calls "incarnational language," namely, "words that resonate with the senses as they aim for the stars" (Norris, p. 699). Rejecting the banal verbiage of sound bites, the incendiary speech of ideologues, and the wearying abstractions of academics, the church must present itself as the schoolhouse of God's word, its textbook, for only it can offer an *enlivening* word, the Word made flesh.

The root of the problem, Qoheleth claims, is that human discourse is characterized more by the bliss of ignorance and denial than by the conviction of true knowledge. It is best not to speak about what one does not know, Qoheleth warns with another rhetorical question (6:12b). Given their limited life span and frail existence, mortals do not know for certain what is good. To know the good is to possess the necessary wherewithal to determine one's life. But that is out of the question and outside the realm of human possibility. The sage claims that no knowledge of absolute goodness can be gained from an ephemeral existence such as ours (cf. Job 8:9). As the sun sets, shadows melt into darkness, and like a shadow, human life returns to dust. As one cannot escape the contingency of human existence, so one cannot apprehend, cognitively or materially, enduring goodness. To do so would be comparable to Adam laying hold of the Tree of Life, from which he was barred (Gen. 3:22–24; cf. Prov. 3:18) or Gilgamesh digesting the plant of rejuvenation (see Introduction). Human life is fleeting, so also human understanding. And to add insult to injury, all life is "vain." It is devoid of ultimate purpose and empty of absolute meaning. The good that

70

avails itself to the living is to be found in the contingencies, not in otherworldly absolutes.

Ecclesiastes 7:1–14
Proverbs of Paradox

Qoheleth presents a series of proverbs that concludes with a bit of advice cast in prose. Although several proverbs are featured prior to this chapter (e.g., 1:15, 18; 2:14; 4:5, 6, 12, 13; 5:1 [Heb. 4:17]), chapter 7 contains the first of three major lists (see 9:17—10:4; 10:8—11:4). Put simplistically, the biblical proverb is a terse and evocative vehicle for imparting instruction. Not confined to the wisdom corpus, proverbs are also attested in narrative material (e.g., Judg. 8:2, 21; 1 Sam. 16:7b; 24:13; 1 Kings 20:11), where they serve a critical role in the plot, frequently resolving conflict between major characters (see Fontaine). More broadly, the proverb plays an indispensable role in regulating social relations and sustaining common values. More than banal truisms, proverbs employ concrete images as metaphors to evoke reflection and prompt prudent or moral action. Frequently, they are situationally specific rather than universal in scope (cf. Prov. 26:4–5). Hence, proverbs are not wholly identical to aphorisms or maxims, and they cannot be locked into a single interpretation or role. Indeed, the power of the proverb lies in its versatility. Depending upon the context, a proverb can generate various meanings and functions.

Although the proverbs featured in the latter half of Ecclesiastes seem at first glance to be listed in random fashion, arranged without rhyme or reason, Qoheleth does provide sufficient clues for determining their contextual message and, ultimately, their place in the larger ethos of the book. Overall, the ancient sage exploits the rhetorical power of the proverb to underscore the paradoxical nature of life, of life filled with mystery and contradiction. The intractable nature of "vanity," or *hebel*, constitutes the broadest context for interpreting Qoheleth's proverbs.

The proverbs that comprise roughly the first half of chapter 7 range from the typically conventional (e.g., vv. 1a, 5–6, 8–9, 11–12) to the radical and enigmatic (e.g., vv. 1b–4, 13). In this list, the form of the "better-than" saying is frequently employed (vv. 1, 2a, 3, 5, 8; see also 4:6, 13; 5:4; 6:9). Although seemingly slapped together, these proverbs evince some continuity in theme and rhetorical movement. The first

71

several proverbs deal with the topic of death and, relatedly, mourning and sorrow (vv. 1b–4). Serving as a transition to the following material and a link to the preceding, verse 4 introduces the morally exclusive categories of the wise and the foolish, a distinction that continues through verse 7. Similarly, verse 8 serves as a transition into the next group of proverbs by echoing the sentiment of verse 1b and commending certain aspects of wise living that are developed in verses 8b–12. These terse observations and exhortations conclude with two prose commands that direct the reader to God's ordering of life (vv. 13–14). Together, verses 1–14 serve to instruct the reader of his or her true humanity within the world of vanity.

The Wisdom of Death (7:1–4)

The first proverb in the series conjoins two unlikely themes: a "good name" and death. The connection is not a natural one. Indeed, the opposite seems more true to form: a person's name is determined *at birth*, not at death. The personal name, particularly in biblical birth stories, determined a person's identity and, in part, reputation (e.g., Gen. 4:25 [Seth]; 5:28–29 [Noah]; 25:25–26 [Esau and Jacob]). The value of a good name or reputation (*šēm*) is, no doubt, of great value, exceeding that of "fine oil" (*šemen*), a clever pun. According to conventional wisdom, fame outlasts wealth (e.g., Prov. 22:1; Sir. 41:11–13). Yet echoing the sentiments of Job and Jeremiah (Job 3:3–26; Jer. 20:14–15), Qoheleth places comparable value upon the "day of death" over and against "the day of birth" (cf. Eccl. 7:2, 8; 9:10; 11:8). How the "day of death" relates exactly to a "good name," however, is enigmatic, an indication of Qoheleth's distinctive stamp on the accumulated wisdom of the sages. But scratch the surface and various possible connections emerge.

Qoheleth is no doubt aware that a person's reputation is not fully established until after death. By declaring that a heroic death will guarantee lasting fame, Gilgamesh exhorts his panic-stricken friend Enkidu to buck up and courageously face the terrible Humbaba (see Introduction). Both the warrior king, Gilgamesh, and the royal sage, Qoheleth, recognize that human glory, if there is such a thing, is essentially a *posthumous* "victory." Death, rather than life, is the sine qua non of a person's reputation and identity. Qoheleth earlier observed in 6:10 that *'ādām*, the name for humanity, connotes weakness before the Almighty, the result of death's invincible power. Regardless of what Qoheleth specifically has in mind in this opening proverb, the sage has dragged conventional wisdom kicking and screaming into the realm of

72

the absurd. His warrant for doing so is the topsy-turvy nature of human existence, in which death, not life, is the measure of all things.

The overall theme of death's primacy over life is developed in the following proverbs, in which Qoheleth expresses a moral preference for mourning over mirth and sorrow over revelry (7:2–4). Whereas much conventional wisdom warns against the debilitating effects of sorrow or despair, which breaks the spirit (Prov. 15:13), "dries up the bones" (17:22), "gnaws the human heart" (25:20b), and tears the soul (27:9), Qoheleth exhorts the reader to embrace sorrow and to enter the "house of mourning." The paradoxical nature of the sage's advice is also found in Prov. 14:13:

> Even in laughter the heart is sad, and the end of joy is grief.

But while this piece of proverbial wisdom poignantly highlights joy's ephemeral nature, Qoheleth's goes further by exhorting the reader to welcome sorrow and to refrain from darkening the entrance to the "house of feasting" or "mirth." This "house" suggests the setting of a wedding ceremony, in which marital love is honored and celebrated. But the sage distances himself from what the Song of Songs, for example, so rapturously commends (e.g., Cant. 5:1). Whereas the love poet depicts a passion that proves fiercer than the grave (8:6–7), the somber sage exposes revelry as an exercise in denial of death's totalizing claim upon life (cf. Eccl. 11:7—12:7). For the sage who has seen it all, the heart-wrenching dirge says something more profound about life than any raucous drinking song. "Like pilgrims to th' appointed place we tend; / The world's an inn, and death the journey's end," the poet John Dryden poignantly notes (quoted in Jacobsen, p. 208).

Two reasons are given for Qoheleth's preference for sorrow, and they cut to the very heart of the book: death is the end for everyone (v. 2b), and true joy is found only through sorrow (v. 3a). Although the irony runs thick, these two proverbs effectively summarize the sage's message about living out one's finitude. The inescapable reality of death is for Qoheleth the point of departure for life (v. 2b). Death orients the self toward authentic, rather than false, living. The end of life is, as it were, the ground of being in Qoheleth's ethic of finitude. Death must be accepted fully, the sage contends, in order to live the good life, however minimal it may seem. Otherwise, life would be a sham, a perpetual state of denial before the inevitable. Joy that is not born of sorrow is artificial. Such an observation is critical to Qoheleth's larger analysis of joy, for it reveals that joy is not simply an antidote to the toilsome task of living, an opium for the toiling masses, as it were. To the contrary, like the phoenix rising from the ashes, true gladness emerges

73

from sorrow (v. 3b). If anything, such joy, born from grief, is resilient to the harsh realities of life, much in contrast to the merriment of fools, whose perception is woefully limited. Without confronting our finitude, Qoheleth claims, we lose our capacity for joy. True joy is found in the wake rather than in the revelry (v. 4).

As noted above, verse 4 injects a conventional dichotomy into the discussion of the relationship between joy and sorrow, namely, the polarity of wisdom and folly. In Hebrew anthropology the "heart" represents the seat of intelligence and volition (cf. 1:13, 17; 2:3; 8:9, 16). The domiciles of "mourning" and "mirth" in which the "heart" resides—the ancient equivalents to the funeral home and the wedding banquet (see v. 2; cf. Jer. 16:5)—have been transformed by Qoheleth into veritable schoolhouses of virtue and vice, respectively. The "house of mourning" has become the wise person's natural setting or element, whereas the fool's habitation is the "house of feasting." In one, the heart is nurtured in the ways of wisdom by being confronted with the end of life (cf. 12:1–7). Qoheleth earlier observed that knowledge and sorrow fit hand-in-glove (1:18). In the other "house," the heart is perverted in the ways of folly. The "house of mirth" is nothing more than a façade whose cloistered walls perpetuate the illusion that pleasure is eternal and ignorance is bliss. This "house of feasting" attempts to shield itself against life's one certain reality, death, but to no avail. The house of mourning, rather, holds the key to life. This paradox is not so enigmatic, bizarre as it might seem. Ask anyone who has worked in a hospice, where the most profound truths of life are laid to heart, and joy and despair are knit together.

The proverb of verse 4 represents a radical transformation of wisdom's natural setting, as described in Proverbs 9:1–6, in which wisdom, as hostess, serves up a lavish banquet for the sake of her would-be disciples. She creates, in effect, a house of feasting. Her nemesis and counterpart in Proverbs 9, the "foolish woman," also invites passersby to her home, where they can partake of "stolen water" and eat bread "in secret," an allusion, in part, to illicit sexual conduct (v. 17). Her house is the façade of Sheol (v. 18). Qoheleth, however, reverses these two domiciles. Wisdom, as embodied by the wise person, inhabits the house of death, whereas the fool's heart is lodged in the house of feasting. Yet this reversal is not without sapiential warrant. Wisdom's house in Proverbs 9 welcomes those who are just beginning the journey of instruction (Prov. 9:4, 6). For Qoheleth, the destination of that journey is the full awareness of death; thus, the entrance to wisdom's house has become, as it were, death's door. But there is no way around this threshold, Qoheleth claims, for any other way offers only a false anti-

74

dote against the harsh realities of life, which must be faced on their own terms. The real feast, Qoheleth concludes, comes only at the funeral (see Tamez, "Living Wisely," 37). And as any pastor knows, the feast of fellowship begins at the gravesite. If the book of Ecclesiastes "has indeed the smell of a tomb about it" (so Robinson, p. 258), then it also bears the unmistakable scent of fried chicken (a typical Southern dish served after the funeral).

Qoheleth reminds the church that faith in Christ entails facing the fullness of death (see the epilogue of the commentary). The hope of the resurrection does not rest on the denial of death, but on the full acceptance of death's all-encompassing scope. As death marks the beginning of wisdom's journey for Qoheleth, so death in baptism marks the beginning of the journey of faith. Christians cannot forget that Christ's victory over death is a costly one, some would even say a pyrrhic victory, one that costs nothing less than life itself: "[U]nless a grain of wheat falls into the earth and dies, it remains just a single grain; but if it dies, it bears much fruit," declares Jesus (John 12:24–25; cf. Mark 8:35).

The Polarity of Wisdom (7:5–7)

Verses 5–7 further underscore the gulf that divides the wise from the foolish, a dichotomy clearly established in conventional wisdom. This section begins by noting the comparative worth of the "rebuke" (*gĕʿârâ*), a technical term for instruction in sapiential rhetoric (e.g., Prov. 13:1, 8; 17:10). Equivalent to "reproof" (*tôkaḥat*), the rebuke of the wise is considered constructive and instructive, despite its harshness of form. Indeed, it constitutes the heart of wisdom's pedagogy (Prov. 19:25; 27:5; 29:15). "The wise, when rebuked, will love you," exhorts wisdom (9:8b). The "one who rejects a rebuke," however, "goes astray" (10:17b). "The scoffer" is by definition one who "does not listen to rebuke" (13:1b; see also 15:12). Comparable to the "two-edged sword" of God's word in Hebrews 4:12, the rebuke of the wise is penetrating as it is edifying: "A rebuke strikes deeper into a discerning person than a hundred blows into a fool" (Prov. 17:10).

Full of narcissistic babble, the "song of fools," by contrast, is noted for its distinct lack of instructive value. Perhaps the fool's discourse is fraught with flattering adoration—the antithesis of the wise rebuke—or intones the drinking songs emanating from the "house of mirth," which drown out life's bitter sorrows (Eccl. 7:2, 4). In any case, Qoheleth commends wisdom's harshest pedagogical form over the useless discourse of fools, which is likened to the sound of brittle thorns being

75

crushed under a pot's weight. The "crackling of thorns" represents the cackling of fools, who are not even aware of their doom ("vanity," v. 6).

The following proverb provides a degree of nuance to the stereo-typical divide that separates the wise and the fool depicted above. Qoheleth acknowledges that there is an unfortunate way by which even the wise can become foolish. Unrelieved "oppression" (cf. 4:1) can turn a discerning mind into senseless mush. Qoheleth earlier noted the pandemic nature of oppression with respect to the poor; it is nothing new (4:1; 5:8). Indeed, much of proverbial wisdom highlights the tragic and offensive nature of oppression (e.g., Prov. 13:23; 22:16, 22–23; 28:3, 16a). But whereas such wisdom rests on an absolute distinction between the wise and the foolish, Qoheleth concedes that there are external conditions in which a wise person is forced to compromise his or her integrity. As Qoheleth has elsewhere remarked, there is more in common between the wise and the foolish than meets the eye; most notably they share a common fate (2:14–16). The ever present possibility of moral compromise among the wise is also recognized by an otherwise unknown biblical sage named Agur, who prays to God that he not be poor, lest he "steal and profane the name of my God" (Prov. 30:9). The trauma of unmitigated oppression can knock a person morally senseless, forcing even the righteous into the mire of turpitude. However, relief from the toil of oppression, as in the form of sustenance and rest, is essential for the cultivation of wisdom and virtue. Wisdom is not the product of desperate measures.

Related to oppression is the corrupting nature of a bribe. Biblical wisdom is actually divided on the usefulness of bribery. On the one hand, a bribe "is like a magic stone in the eyes of those who give it; wherever they turn, they prosper" (Prov. 17:8); it "opens doors" and "gives access to the great" (18:16). On the other hand, the bribe is the property of the wicked, who "pervert the ways of justice" (17:23). Perversion, indeed, is precisely what Qoheleth sees in receiving a bribe (Eccl. 7:7). A bribe may open doors and bring about prosperity for the one who gives it, but it also perverts the heart of the one who accepts it. According to deuteronomic justice, a bribe "blinds the eyes of the wise and subverts the cause of those who are in the right" (Deut. 16:19). Bribery leads to partiality, which undermines the foundations of justice.

Living for the End in the Now (7:8–12)

76

Whereas the first section of proverbs, emphasizing the reality of death and the virtue of sorrow, highlights the negative implications of Qoheleth's ethic of finitude, verse 8 introduces a new unit that focuses on the positive aspects of living in view of the "end." Recalling verse 1b, verse 8a gives preference to the "end of a thing" over "its beginning" or genesis. Qoheleth commends an outlook that holds the end of an object or subject firmly in view. Perhaps that is why Qoheleth strips all language of *creation* from his view of the cosmos, which opens the book (1:3–8), while depicting so forcefully the end of life at the book's conclusion (12:2–7). In any case, the sage is not espousing a standard ethic of teleology, a way of life oriented around purpose. The "end" of something is not its goal; it is simply its termination. Better it is to realize that generations go into oblivion than to celebrate their coming (cf. 1:4). Such a forward-looking perspective is far from optimistic. To the contrary, it constitutes a sobering, realistic outlook that takes account of the temporal nature and demise of all things. Such an orientation, however, undergirds rather than undermines certain positive elements found in conventional wisdom. Qoheleth's outlook gives preferential value, for example, to patience over arrogance and anger (7:8b–9; see Prov. 12:16; 16:32; 25:15; 29:11; 30:33). Patience is cultivated and impulsive behavior is contained by the full awareness of the end of existence.

The sage's end perspective also counters the temptation of nostalgia, of glorifying the past at the expense of the present (Eccl. 7:10; cf. 5:20 [Heb. v. 19]). This verse allegedly contains a quote from Qoheleth's audience. In their rhetorical question, the sage's listeners voice a preference for the past, which Qoheleth finds sapientially objectionable. In a rapidly changing world, both economically and culturally, the nostalgic longing for the past was, no doubt, a popular, if not natural, response. Cast as it is, the question is a veritable lament of the present. But to devalue the present in light of the past is anathema for Qoheleth. The sage is not suggesting that the present is any improvement over the past. "There is nothing new under the sun," he intones elsewhere. Qoheleth is, rather, addressing the underlying issue of motivation and conduct. Regardless of whether the present is fraught with less favorable conditions, the present constitutes the immediate realm of the living, from which one cannot and should not try to escape. The present moment carries a morally binding force all its own. Wisdom informs the living of *these* days, not the reliving of the "former days." All one can seize is the present, not the past or, for that matter, the future.

That wisdom is informative and beneficial for the living of these days is developed in the subsequent proverbs, but not without a degree of irony. Wisdom, the proverb of 7:11 acknowledges, gives its recipient a certain edge in life, comparable to an inheritance. It is noteworthy, as Seow notes (*Ecclesiastes*, p. 249), that this proverb deliberately breaks from the typical "better-than" pattern that characterizes the proverbs of verses 1, 2, 3, 5, and 8. Wisdom is no better than wealth (cf. Prov. 3:14; 8:11, 19; 16:16). Given his negative evaluation of wealth elsewhere (Eccl. 5:13–17 [Heb. vv. 12–16]), Qoheleth is not so much elevating wealth as demoting wisdom. Yet the sage does accord wisdom a measure of relative advantage (yōtēr; 7:11b) for "those who see the sun," that is, for the living (cf. 9:10). Moreover, in the following verse, the gain (yitrôn) offered by knowledge is claimed to preserve the life of the one who possesses knowledge (v. 12b). An apparent tension, however, arises from Qoheleth's denunciations elsewhere of the efficacy of net gain (e.g., 1:3; 2:11; 3:9; 6:10–12). For all the advantage in life that it seems to offer (cf. Prov. 3:13–18), wisdom cannot ensure lasting gain. Yet wisdom, the sage affirms, has its use on this side of life, as does money, by enhancing, however minimally, the quality of life in the face of mounting absurdity. Wisdom, in fact, is better than folly in the same way that sorrow is better than laughter (v. 3a). Only through wisdom can one discover the relative value of the present and the enjoyment that it offers within an existence that is globally marked by absurdity.

These last two verses indicate a subtle but nonetheless significant shift in the larger discussion of biblical wisdom. Contrary to proverbial wisdom, Qoheleth nowhere claims that wisdom exceeds the value of wealth. "My fruit is better than gold, even fine gold, and my yield than choice silver," proclaims wisdom in Prov. 8:19 (see also 3:14; 8:11; 16:16). By contrast, Qoheleth equates the "protection of wisdom" with the "protection of money" (literally "in the shade of" wisdom/money). One comes to possess wisdom as one acquires wealth; both require cultivation. Their equivalency, however, departs from conventional wisdom, which takes pains to distinguish wisdom from material wealth without entirely severing their interconnections. Solomon, for example, was granted wisdom by God because he prayed for a discerning heart rather than for prosperity and the defeat of his enemies (1 Kings 3:11–12). Yet he was also granted unprecedented wealth by virtue of his "selfless" desire for wisdom (v. 13). Similarly, wisdom promises her disciples that not only will they lead lives of righteousness and justice, they will also be enriched (Prov. 8:20–21).

Qoheleth has, in effect, materialized wisdom, reducing it without rejecting its modestly salutary worth. Like money, a person can use wisdom to his or her benefit; like wealth, it can be lost in a bad investment (Eccl. 5:14). As Qoheleth claims elsewhere (7:23–24), wisdom can slip through one's fingers as easily as money can be illicitly transferred from owner to stranger (2:18–19; 6:2). Wisdom is the proverbial lost coin.

What God Has Wrought (7:13–14)

These two verses round out this section with explicitly theological statements. Perhaps echoing the quotation in 1:10 ("See this is new"), Qoheleth directs the reader's attention to the "work of God" and complements it with a rhetorical question stressing the perdurability of what God has wrought (see also 3:14). Qoheleth had made a similar statement in 1:15a, but with one notable difference. Here, the sage directly mentions God as the fashioner of the "crooked." Implied is the absolute disjunction between divine and human perception (cf. 1 Sam. 16:7). What appears crooked to human beings may be divinely sanctioned, created by God, no less, and thus impervious to human correction or judgment.

The Bible is filled with accounts of divine activity contravening human expectations and norms. Job's encounter with the God of the whirlwind is a classic case in point. The creator showcases the denizens of the wild for Job's edification, revealing their inherent dignity and worth in the face of Job's harbored disgust for these animals and what they represent (Job 38:39—41:34 [Heb. v. 26]). What Job viewed with contempt and horror, God depicts as objects of personal care and affirmation. Job's world, consequently, becomes radically disoriented (Brown, *The Ethos of the Cosmos*, pp. 360–75). The Isaiah of the exile proclaims the radically new thing of God's redemptive activity, which entails the designation of a foreigner, the Persian king Cyrus, to be Israel's shepherd and "messiah" (Isa. 44:28; 45:1). Peter receives a vision from God that displays a host of unclean animals, which God commands him to eat, leaving him with the message, "What God has made clean, you must not call profane" (Acts 10:9–16). Amos admonishes his people for desiring the "day of the Lord" and assuming it to be a time of deliverance and vindication, whereas in reality it is a day of "darkness, not light" (Amos 5:18–20).

In each case, God defies human expectation. The adage "The Lord works in mysterious ways" most certainly applies. And Qoheleth applies the inscrutability of God's creative work against the human presumption to categorize and thereby control what goes on under the sun. Created by God, even what is "crooked" is invested with a dignity that commands acceptance, if not respect, in place of contempt and correction. Qoheleth's proverb, in short, acknowledges the limitations of human judgment and the inefficacy of human activity before the throne of sovereignty.

God, moreover, is the creator of both the "day of adversity" or misfortune and that of "prosperity." Joy is the appropriate response to the

79

latter day. The day of misfortune provokes an awareness that mortals are profoundly limited, irredeemably finite in both knowledge and power. They cannot dispute with the one who is stronger (6:11) and in their finitude are kin to the animals (3:18–19). Their place is to welcome the good with joy and accept adversity when it comes, both wrought by God, according to Qoheleth. The human subject can only take what comes and no more. To defy the bad in bitter protest, as Job does, only tears the self in anger, Bildad observes (Job 18:4). In contrast to the "impatient" Job of the poetic cycles, the Job of the prologue acts in a very Qohelethian way: "Shall we receive the good at the hand of God, and not receive the bad?" (2:10). That God creates both bane and blessing serves as a check on human presumption and, in turn, boundless ambition. God is in heaven; humans are stuck on earth (Eccl. 5:2 [Heb. v. 1]). Rather than allowing chaos to wreak uncontrolled havoc on creation, God firmly holds the pendulum as it swings from shalom to misery and invariably back again (3:1–8).

Ecclesiastes 7:15–29
The Primacy of Reverence and the Relativity of Wisdom

A new section begins with a new observation. Qoheleth now refers to his own life as utterly "vain," bereft of any knowledge of the future (see above) and devoid of ultimate significance. Nevertheless, his purview is thoroughly global: "I have seen everything." And what he sees is the offense of offenses, the reversal of moral character. In 3:16, the sage noted the subjugation of justice and righteousness by wickedness. Here, Qoheleth finds righteousness inefficacious for the righteous and wickedness edifying to evildoers. Righteousness and wickedness are more than abstract moral qualities; they are settings or spheres of existence in which the human agent acts and gains identity. They are, in short, character domains. Traditionally, righteousness is the salutary sphere of moral agency, but no longer within Qoheleth's purview. It seems that righteousness and wickedness have traded places in the absurd scheme of things (cf. 8:14).

The Presumption of Righteousness (7:15–22)

80

Qoheleth makes the startling claim that righteousness, like folly, can hasten one's death (vv. 15, 17). The sage finds hopelessly naive and, in fact, contravened by experience the assertion that "righteousness delivers from death" (Prov. 11:4; see also 10:2; 3:16). To the contrary, excessive righteousness, paralleled by immoderate wisdom, proves to be risky business. Yet there is a lesson to be learned: the way of righteousness and wisdom is not the fanatic's trek. Such rabid conduct will only lead to self-devastation. The same, however, also goes for foolish behavior, which is deemed eminently hazardous to one's livelihood. Extending his observation that the wicked and the righteous suffer similar fates (Eccl. 2:14, 3:14–20), Qoheleth's reflections in 7:16–18 likely draw from an older proverbial tradition that prescribes moderate behavior, as found among the Aramaic proverbs of Ahiqar:

> Do not be too sweet, lest you be swallowed;
> Do not be too bitter, lest you be spat out. (see Lindenberger, p. 149)

Qoheleth has, in effect, moralized this pithy saying by claiming that the extremes of virtue and vice lead invariably to self-ruin and premature death. Neither path by itself leads to lasting gain; rather, they must somehow be balanced against each other (see Crenshaw, pp. 140–41).

Qoheleth reveals the "virtuous" extreme for what it is, namely, a matter of arrogant presumption. Absolute righteousness, like global wisdom, remains essentially unreachable (see 7:23–24). To think and act otherwise reflects an exalted estimation of one's moral faculties, which will result only in disappointment and ruin. Analogous to the situation of obsessive toil, absolute righteousness is exposed for its inability to ensure long life and happiness (cf. Prov. 3:16). Accompanied by the lofty expectations of reward, the pretense of blamelessness will result only in utter despair, if not self-destruction. The grandiose exercise of righteousness invites only the self's undoing.

Like Job, Qoheleth severs the alleged causal nexus between righteousness and prosperity, countering the extreme, albeit logical, conclusion that *ultra*righteousness, *a fortiori*, will afford ultimate fulfillment. Qoheleth exposes all efforts to fulfill the absolute ideals of righteousness as self-serving attempts to reap glory. A life obsessed with righteousness, in fact, blinds a person from his or her own sinfulness. Righteousness that leads to self-righteousness is a delusion, for no one can claim a sinless existence, Qoheleth contends (7:20; cf. Matt. 7:3–5). Righteousness is not a proving ground for the monumentally fit. Moreover, pure righteousness is obsessed with the patriarchal trappings of honor and communal esteem, qualities that exist only through social consensus but can be easily undercut by any slave who happens to mutter a curse against the honoree, the master (Eccl. 7:21). Such obsession with outward acknowledgment reflects an inward delusion

81

regarding the putative efficacy of one's "purity" in thought and conduct. Ultrarighteousness, in short, takes root and flourishes in the soil of presumption. Yet in bursting the bubble of righteous pretension, Qoheleth cautions against considering the other extreme, namely, the folly of wickedness. Wickedness, too, will result in one's untimely demise. Elsewhere, Qoheleth determined that the ultimate fates of the wise and of the fool were one and the same (1:14–15); now he is acutely aware that to excel in either wisdom or folly only hastens that fate.

Qoheleth suggests an alternative to these two extremes, and it is found in his implicit commendation of divine reverence (v. 18b; see also 5:7 [Heb. v. 6]; 8:12b). Godly fear forges a middle ground, but not as some muddled mean, as if righteousness should be tempered with a modicum of wickedness, or folly mitigated with a healthy dose of wisdom. Reverence is neither a matter of fanatical fear that raises the bar of moral conduct to unattainable or obsessive levels, nor a matter of indifference or moral complacency. Rather, the fear of God is based on an acute awareness of human finitude and a realistic assessment of life's vicissitudes. Again, no righteous person is without blemish, Qoheleth observes (7:20), and the negative lessons of wickedness and extreme righteousness must accompany the moral self in all conduct.

Like baggage items of equal weight, these lessons must be carried, one in each hand, in order to walk straight, eschewing fanaticism, on the one hand, and folly, on the other. The result is a salutary balance in conduct and reverence. The one who succeeds is the one who is able, literally, to "go forth" (*yēṣēʾ;* NRSV "succeed"), to proceed resolutely on the path of life, on the way of wisdom stripped of its glorious promises of ultimate fulfillment but retaining, nonetheless, a level of salutary benefits, however minimal. Wisdom is no longer the street paved with gold, as Qoheleth's predecessors had contended, but it remains a straight, albeit unassuming, path, with its own relative goods. And that is as good as wisdom gets. Wisdom retains a positive value even in a world fraught with political absurdity (see v. 19).

Subsisting on Sapientia (7:23–29)

The kind of wisdom that is intimately associated with the tree or fountain of life in Proverbs (e.g., 11:30; 13:12, 14) proves to be unattainable for the sage. Serving as both the method and object of Qoheleth's investigation, wisdom remains too remote and deep for access. The language recalls the pivotal chapter in Job on the elusiveness of wisdom. "Where shall wisdom be found?" initiates the inquiry (Job

28:12). "Who can find it out?" Qoheleth asks rhetorically. The answer in Job is fraught with mystery.

> It is hidden from the eyes of all living,
>   and concealed from the birds of the air.
> Abaddon and Death say,
>   "We have heard a rumor of it with our ears."
> God understands the way to it,
>   and he knows its place.
>
> (Job 28:21–23)

As (erstwhile?) king and sage (see Eccl. 1:17; 2:12), Qoheleth took it upon himself to seek out a wisdom powerful enough to explain the world, to explicate the "sum of things" (*hešbôn;* 7:25, 27), and to expose once and for all the folly of wickedness. But it was all for naught. There are some things that remain ever hidden from human discernment, including something as central and integral to human reflection as wisdom.

In his searching, the sage nevertheless arrives at a certain level of perception; he has "found" something that confirms the madness of folly. In his quest for knowledge, a human figure of horrific proportion looms before him, blocking the sage's path; she is none other than "the woman who is a trap" (7:26). She is not to be identified with womankind in general. (The definite article ["*the* woman"] suggests that the following clause is syntactically restrictive.) Rather, a *particular* gendered figure, indeed one of mythic proportions, serves as the root of Qoheleth's fear and contempt. She is the "strange woman" or "foolish woman" portrayed in the book of Proverbs. Known primarily for her role as a seductive adulteress and as folly personified, she is the antithesis to woman wisdom (Prov. 2:16–19; 5:3–6; 7:6–27; 9:13–18). The expressed mission of this *femme fatale* is to entice clueless youths to engage in extramarital sex, luring them ultimately to their doom (7:21–27). Her domicile is the façade of Sheol. Her hapless victim "follows her, and goes like an ox to the slaughter, or bounds like a stag toward the trap, . . . like a bird rushing into a snare, not knowing that it will cost him his life" (vv. 22–23). Echoing the sage's word, a father warns his son in Proverbs, "Do not desire her beauty in your heart, and do not let her capture you with her eyelashes" (6:25). For Qoheleth, only the "one who pleases God" (literally "is good before God"; cf. Eccl. 2:26) can escape the wiles of this dangerous woman.

Why Qoheleth marks this woman—indeed, any woman at all—as the source of his fear and contempt warrants further exploration, particularly since this biblical text, among others, can easily be appropriated in ways that dehumanize women. To state the obvious, the language of the ancient male sage draws from the chauvinistic mentality of his time, cultivated within a patriarchal culture from which even biblical Israel was not immune. From the ancient male perspective, the other gender not infrequently represented sin and social threat (see also Sir. 25:13–26). Qoheleth was no exception. Indeed, Eccl. 7:28b, which esteems the male over and against the female, even if by a little, is misogynistic to the core. While a righteous man can be found among a cast of thousands, a woman of comparable moral mettle is nowhere to be seen. However, Qoheleth himself probably cannot take credit for this statement. The distinctive language and intrusive style of this half verse vis-à-vis its literary context (e.g., the use of 'ādām to denote male gender—contra its inclusive sense throughout the rest of the book— and the convoluted use of the word "found") indicate its secondary nature, as others have shown (see Seow, *Ecclesiastes*, pp. 264–65). Again, Qoheleth's negative focus is not on female nature per se (cf. 9:9), but on the mytho-horrific figure of personified folly, a fatal attraction from the androcentric purview. Whereas woman wisdom and her nemesis, woman stranger, are given equal and opposite roles in Proverbs 1—9, Qoheleth finds a disturbing imbalance between these two mythic personifications: while wisdom recedes into oblivion, becoming "far off and deep," personified folly looms all the larger before him. It is her presence that stops Qoheleth almost dead in his tracks.

Qoheleth's ostensibly failed search, nevertheless, yields something of a discovery. The sage concludes that God is not to blame for human failings (Eccl. 7:29). Although human beings are created "straightforward" or "right" (*yāšār*), they are inclined to seek out "many schemes" or inventions (*ḥiššĕbōnôt*, a word play on *ḥešbôn* ["sum" or "inventory"; vv. 25, 27]). Formulated proverbially, Qoheleth identifies a perverseness that cannot be attributed to God but, rather, ascribed to human invention. Human "inventions," furthermore, are rooted in false and self-destructive "accountings" of life and conduct. A certain irony is evident in comparison with verse 13, in which the sage acknowledges crookedness as an intractable part of God's handiwork and straightness as a distinctly human preoccupation or obsession. But as for humankind's *created* (i.e., intrinsic) nature, straight and upright is the baseline (v. 29). Yet, for whatever reason, human beings have demonstrated time and again a proclivity toward devising a multitude of machinations, much to their own harm. The primal couple's disobedience in the garden, which the sage likely has in mind, is only the first example. Indeed, their disobedience, deluded by a false sense of knowledge, according to Genesis 2—3, unleashed the fragmenting forces of alienation and inequity into the relational equation. Rather than achieving divine glory, as promised by the cunning serpent, the primal man and woman encountered shame and curse, pain and alienation, a toilsome existence (3:7–24). Such was the first failed "scheme," to adopt the sage's language. Another, not unrelated, example of misdirected thinking is the presumed inferior status of women, a patriarchal "invention" in which even Qoheleth, the man, was complicit.

Qoheleth has found that his noble quest for wisdom is but another scheme, one among many that mortals fervently devise in their delusion. As Adam worked the rocky soil by the sweat of his brow in order to subsist, so Qoheleth toils in his quest for wisdom and the "sum of things" but is never quite successful. The sage can only subsist on the traces of a wisdom beyond his ken. Qoheleth is left, on the one hand, with grave disillusionment and, on the other, with a profound recognition of humanity's self-limitation before the mystery of it all, an awareness that ultimately fosters an appreciation for humble simplicity in one's life and conduct. It is this realization of humanity's finitude that somehow makes all the toil necessary, perhaps even worthwhile. In any case, toil is humanity's lot, as it was for Adam (cf. Eccl. 3:22; 5:18–19 [Heb. vv. 17–18]; 9:10).

Ecclesiastes 8:1–9

The Limits of Power

As Qoheleth complains of the multitude of schemes conjured up by human beings, he also observes their woeful limitations. The limited exercise of human power, whether to discern a matter or affect the course of history, is the theme that unifies this section.

Qoheleth opens with a rhetorical question regarding the alleged incomparability of the sage: "Who is like the wise [person]?" By itself, this proverb stresses the unmatchable uniqueness of the discerning person. However, in its larger context it suggests that the sage is more than just a rarity. No one is capable of appropriating wisdom any more than someone can know "the interpretation of a thing" (see, e.g., 7:23–24). Such sentiment is also shared by the biblical sage Agur.

> Surely I am too stupid to be human;
>   I do not have human understanding.
> I have not learned wisdom,
>   nor have I knowledge of the holy ones.
>   (Prov. 30:2–3)

85

Both Qoheleth and Agur share a profound sense of sapiential limitation. Whereas Agur laments his lack of knowledge of divine matters, Qoheleth admits ignorance over the "interpretation" or solution of any matter. All of life, from the particular to the globally abstract, is impenetrably deep for even the most discerning. It is all the work of an inscrutable God (8:17). Qoheleth is no Daniel, the consummate interpreter of dreams and enigmatic handwritings (Dan. 2:45; 5:15).

Yet—and there is always a "yet" in Qoheleth's logic (see Introduction)—wisdom does have its value. Wisdom elicits a pleasant demeanor (literally "causes one's face to shine"), softening any hardness or severity of countenance (Eccl. 8:1b). A shining face conveys favor and indicates a gracious spirit. Elsewhere in biblical tradition, it is God who causes the face to shine (e.g., Num. 6:25; Pss. 31:16; 67:1; 80:3, 7, 19; 119:135; Dan. 9:17). Here, wisdom is the source of a cheerful disposition, but as Qoheleth has suggested elsewhere, the change in one's countenance may be only cosmetic, for wisdom is also accompanied by much "vexation" and "sorrow" (Eccl. 1:18). Again, one must keep in mind that proverbs do not necessarily impart universal truths; they are more often situationally oriented. Given its context, particularly in light of the subsequent section, the proverb of 8:1b works: wisdom is indeed the necessary source of a pliant disposition in matters that specifically concern the king and, by extension, God. More broadly, the proverb confirms that through wisdom the import of joy is discerned.

Qoheleth exhorts the reader to obey the king without question or hesitation because of a "sacred oath" or covenant. The sage does not, however, condone a posture of terror; rather, he espouses humble servility (8:3). The king's word is sovereign, his rule incontestable, analogous to the Deity (v. 4). Indeed, Job employs similar terminology to describe God's overpowering will: "He snatches away; who can stop him? Who will say to him, 'What are you doing?'" (Job 9:12). The king can no more be challenged than God's will can be contested, although that is precisely what Job attempts to do. Qoheleth, however, harbors neither the righteous anger nor the chutzpah to mount a verbal assault against the decrees of the king, heavenly or earthly. Compliance reigns by virtue of a "sacred oath" (literally "an oath of God"; cf. Exod. 22:9; 2 Sam. 21:7; 1 Kings 2:43). The incontestable power of the king obfuscates any attempt to understand, let alone defy, the royal command. Instead, the lowly sage (and former king!) advocates simple obedience, not unlike what is urged in Prov. 24:21–22:

My child, fear the LORD and the king,
    And do not disobey either of them;

> For disaster comes from them suddenly,
>   And who knows the ruin that both can bring?

Obedience before the one who is "stronger" (see Eccl. 6:10) is a mark of prudence. Indeed, Qoheleth underscores a certain security in such conduct (8:5). Paul similarly exhorts the church in Rome to "be subject to the governing authorities; for there is no authority except from God" (Rom. 13:1). For Paul, similar to the ancient sage, obedience to the ruling authority rests on a sacral relationship: the reigning authority is a "servant of God" (v. 4). For Qoheleth, however, such sacred civility is more pragmatically oriented.

Wisdom for the sage serves to foster an attitude of compliance before the one who holds the reins of power. Compared to the king's might, the subject's power is of mere relative extent, all the more so before the Almighty. Before omniscience, only calm deference is warranted (see also Eccl. 10:4). In addition, the discerning person knows that every incident under heaven has its "time and way" (literally "time and judgment" [*mišpāṭ*]; see 3:11); such an awareness fosters an attitude of acceptance as well as a level of awareness that is, however, easily obfuscated by the "troubles of mortals," the evil machinations to which human beings are so inclined (see 7:29).

Yet for all that can be understood by those who are wise and "straightforward," not even the wisest can discern the future (8:7). And without such knowledge, humanity is left without power over either breath or death (v. 8). Life-breath (*rûaḥ*) and death cannot be comprehended, much less apprehended and controlled, as if they were commodities to be manipulated. There is no "discharge," or privilege of substitution (see Seow, *Ecclesiastes,* pp. 282–83), from the battle against death, and wickedness, most certainly, is no defense. Not even the king, be he wicked or righteous, holds the power to avert death. Neither righteousness nor wickedness has any effect in warding off death's encroachment upon the living (see also 12:1–8; but cf. Prov. 10:2; 11:4; 12:28; 13:14).

In short, Qoheleth provides both a realistic assessment of royal power and a survivalist's guide for conducting oneself before such power (see also Prov. 23:1–3). However, underlying his advice—in contrast to Paul's "civil theology" in Romans 13—is a cynical awareness of the human tendency to abuse power, particularly in the form of economic control (Eccl. 8:9). Qoheleth acknowledges that kings, and indeed anyone who holds authority over another, tend to wield their power at the expense of others. The exercise of authority, royal or otherwise, consistently bears a destructive potential, the sage observes (see also 5:8 [Heb. v. 7]). Elsewhere, Qoheleth condemns the kind of authority that illicitly transfers one's rightful possessions or inheritance to a stranger (2:18–19; 6:2).

More broadly, the sage acknowledges the pervasiveness of oppression under the sun, a condition directly attributable to the "power" lorded by some, much to the detriment of others (8:9; see also 4:1). Such is the lamentable state of affairs that is all too familiar to society, whether ancient or modern, in which there lacks an advocate who can act on behalf of the dispossessed, one who is willing to stand in the breach and exercise power to counter power. It is precisely because of the lack of power that Qoheleth advocates compliance before the all-powerful king. To do otherwise would be dangerously imprudent. As much as nature abhors a vacuum, a society based on royal authority views any hint of defiance as a blemish to be extirpated. Any resistance, Qoheleth notes with resignation, will prove self-destructive.

Ecclesiastes 8:10–17
The Vanity of Character and the Mystery of God

Inextricably tied to his previous observations, Qoheleth directs his attention to an example of societal injustice, namely the esteem of the wicked and the castigation of the righteous. He first notes the pompously proper burial of the wicked, an offense to his sensibility and an indication of society's misguided esteem. It is "vanity" (v. 10, cf. v. 14b). More generally, the sage laments the loathsome reversal of status among the righteous and the wicked: while the wicked are esteemed as upstanding citizens, the righteous are treated as miscreants (v. 14). In a society that is unable to recognize—much less honor—the righteous, justice is jettisoned, and the capacity for moral outrage has died. Without the swift exercise of due punishment, the human proclivity to do evil looms large (literally "the heart of humanity is filled . . . to do evil"; v. 11). Consequently, any degree of esteem accorded the wicked indicates a systemic moral blindness.

Qoheleth complains of a society in which character counts for nothing, in which the opposite poles of the character spectrum are effectively reversed. While another sage complains of certain social reversals that would cause the earth to "tremble," such as a slave becoming king (Prov. 30:21–23), Qoheleth observes a more systemic travesty, one that fills him with an *odium tremendum* ("awful hatred") yet drives him to a sense of the *mysterium tremendum* ("awesome mystery"). From misery to mystery the sage moves, perhaps all too easily. Despite the rampant inversions of justice, Qoheleth insists on holding on to a life of reverence, of "fearing God" against the odds. Even though the wicked prosper, the sage does not give up hope that holy reverence has its salutary consequences. Here, Qoheleth's stance is entrenched in the ethos of piety. "Here I stand," the sage in effect declares. The God-fearers, Qoheleth insists, will receive some benefit, although Qoheleth does not specify what that benefit might be. In 7:15–18, the sage enjoined a life of avoiding extremes on both ends of the moral spectrum, concluding that with this wisdom of moderation the individual can resolutely "go forth," confident in his or her integrity. Perhaps therein lies the reward.

In both 7:15–18 and 8:10–13, Qoheleth makes the case that indulgence in wickedness increases the likelihood of an untimely demise. In the latter passage, Qoheleth categorically states that the wicked are unable to lengthen their days, which are "like a shadow." Yet the sage also notes the wicked's untimely long life. In the face of this contradiction, Qoheleth's point emerges: it is not by wickedness that the wicked prolong their lives (see 7:17; 8:8b). Such "lengthening of days" for the wicked happens purely by chance in a morally skewed world (see 9:11). In an ethically credible setting, the righteous would prosper and the wicked suffer. Yet even in Qoheleth's topsy-turvy world, rife with contradiction, the sage refuses to let go of his faith in holy reverence. Indeed, the sage acknowledges a self-fortifying element to such "fear." The wicked lack such fear; hence, their existence remains "shadowy." The godly, however, can robustly, even defiantly, "go forth" in a world fraught with moral absurdity.

Along with reverence, Qoheleth exhorts enjoyment (v. 15; see also 2:24–26; 3:12–13, 22; 5:18–20 [Heb. vv. 17–19]; 7:14). Given the moral confusion of a world that is unable to distinguish the ethical from the manifestly immoral, the sage calls for a narrowing of one's moral purview from self-righteous grandiosity to self-fulfilling simplicity, for "there is nothing better." As earlier, Qoheleth combines the simple gifts of sustenance and work, but he cements their mutual relationship here. Eating, drinking, and enjoyment shall "accompany them in their toil." Finding enjoyment *in* one's work, as Qoheleth commends elsewhere, is made possible by finding the proper rhythm of rest *and* work, of toil and refreshment. Decisive is the lack of any reference to profit, much less ambition, in his commendation. Hope for profit drives one into the downward, vicious cycle of all-consuming toil, sapping a person's strength and destroying one's capacity to enjoy life (see 2:22–25; 5:13–20 [Heb. vv. 12–19]).

89

Having effectively severed all meaningful connection between toil and profit, Qoheleth makes painfully clear that gain (or hope for gain) is incapable of rendering work meaningful. Rather, it is the balance between toil and play, between labor and rest, that makes for satisfying work (see the epilogue of the commentary). The joy that he commends, however, is more than an antidote for toil, since Qoheleth finds enjoyment and intrinsic value in work itself. Elsewhere, the sage commends devotion to one's work, for toil resides exclusively in the land of the living, not in Sheol (9:10). The positive value of work emerges when labor is set within the formative context of rest, refreshment, and fellowship (see 4:9).

Concluding his observations on the vanity of character and the necessity of joy, Qoheleth affirms the impenetrable mystery of wisdom and work (8:16–17). His complaint over the moral confusion that besets the world leads him to the impenetrable mystery of divine providence. All that is "happening under the sun" corresponds to God's work (v. 17). The significance of activity, whether on earth or in heaven, is lost. Try as they might, even by forgoing the blissful stupor of sleep, mortals are unable to fathom God's ways and discern wisdom's contours on the rugged landscape of human existence. Qoheleth identifies the consuming goal for which the sages toil: the discernment of God's way in the world. His quest for wisdom is thoroughly theocentric. But like gain, earnestly sought after by all, such wisdom remains ever elusive. All claims to full and certain knowledge are rendered false, for what seems to count toward gaining a glimmer of understanding is invariably countered by a contravening observation. Contradiction rules in all experience under the sun.

Qoheleth's skeptical view on attaining theological knowledge should, if anything, give people of faith, and theologians in particular, pause for thought. That "the Lord works in mysterious ways" is not an empty cliché for Qoheleth. Mystery is endemic to the Deity, Qoheleth claims, and it is this same mystery with which all life "under the sun" is fraught. Qoheleth has observed that for every course of action in one direction, there occurs in due time an accompanying opposite reaction, a sort of Newtonian approach to moral valuation. Indeed, time itself is structured by such polarities (3:1–8). God has made the day of *shalom* and the day of adversity (7:14). The incessant oscillations between the good and the bad that comprise what is "done under the sun," accompanied by the countless absurdities of human conduct, serve to veil the Almighty from all human perception and knowledge. God's intentions and purposes are shrouded in secrecy in the triumphs and travails of life. Qoheleth's statement "God is in heaven and you upon earth" (5:2a

90

[Heb. v. 1a]) illustrates the gulf that divides the Transcendent from the mundane. And while it entails spareness of speech in its immediate context (v. 2b [Heb. v. 1a]), Qoheleth's theology leads more broadly to humble confession of humanity's finitude and limited discernment, a bitter pill that even the wisest of the wise must swallow.

Ecclesiastes 9:1–10
Death and the Moral of the Moment

This central section marks both a culmination of the sage's observations about life before an inscrutable God and a move toward establishing their ethical implications in a comprehensive way. The opening verse marks Qoheleth's attempt to analyze the plethora of his experiences, laying it all to "heart," the seat of intelligence and will in Hebrew anthropology. First and foremost, Qoheleth posits that God alone determines the character and conduct of the righteous. But the rationales behind certain modes of conduct, such as love and hatred, remain unfathomable to mortals (see 3:8a). As elsewhere, Qoheleth considers this situation of human indeterminacy a travesty; "vanity" is the sage's damning verdict upon all that is done under the sun. Life is futile because regardless of what one does or is, the same fate applies. Qoheleth lists several examples of extremes to underscore the absurdity of it all. It is irrelevant whether one is righteous or wicked, good or evil, clean or unclean, whether one regularly offers sacrifice or not (cf. 5:1 [Heb. 4:17]). It does not matter whether one utters vows or not (cf. 5:4–5 [Heb. vv. 3–4]). In the end, all suffer the same fate. Moral distinctions count for nothing before indiscriminate death. The sage does not mince words when he claims that it is all an outrageous "evil" (9:3a). Such is Qoheleth's indictment against a world that offers nothing more than a tomb to die in.

To add insult to injury, there is also an "evil" or "madness" that infects every human heart (v. 3b). By juxtaposing these two levels of evil, external and internal, Qoheleth suggests a causal relationship between the indiscriminate nature of fate and the madness that can beset every human being. In 8:11, the sage complained of the ineffectual execution of punitive justice, which leads to the corruption of the human heart. Now, on a far grander scale, the fate that is universal yet to which most human beings are seemingly oblivious—death—permits a madness to take root in the human heart that compels one to shirk all sense of

91

responsibility. Such is the outcome of hopeless despair. Without accountability, the heart of darkness thrives before it dies.

It is at this point the reader might expect the embittered sage to throw up his hands and admit defeat in the toilsome task of living. But Qoheleth refuses to be overwhelmed with despair. The sage who has seen everything comes to admit that there is something positive in life, even as he peers deep into the yawning chasm of death. Qoheleth is not ready to jump. Instead, the pendulum begins to swing in the other direction. Qoheleth concedes a "hope" (or better "trust" [Seow, *Ecclesiastes,* p. 300]) among the living (v. 4), which he expresses in the evocative proverb, "a living dog is better [off] than a dead lion."

Associated with royal might and prowess in conflict, the lion was considered the archetypal predator, the model of a king from the kingdom of the wild, this "king of beasts." But the lion's regal stature is worthless in death, Qoheleth observes; a dead lion is nothing more than a carcass, fit for the vultures. The dog, by contrast, was typically associated with filth and even death in ancient Near Eastern culture. Moreover, "dog" was frequently a term of contempt in biblical tradition (e.g., 1 Sam. 17:43; Ps. 22:16, 20; Matt. 15:26–27) and remains so in English. "Like a dog that returns to its vomit is a fool who reverts to his folly" (Prov. 26:11; 2 Peter 2:22). The lion and the dog are emblematic of opposing reputations: intelligence and folly, might and weakness, majesty and lowliness. According to the sages of convention, reputation is the individual's lasting legacy for future generations; it is the immortalized self. But for Qoheleth, the groveling dog holds an absolute advantage over the lion's carcass. Life cannot be lived for the sake of the future. A dog at least receives the crumbs that fall from heaven (see Matt. 15:27).

The upshot is that life holds an advantage over death, and that advantage is the certain knowledge of death, a paradoxical hope, to be sure. The "hope" of the living begins with the awareness of death's certitude and points toward those opportunities that avail themselves within the vain brevity of life, particularly the few and fleeting moments of joy. The living are blessed with the *knowledge* of their impending death, while the dead "know nothing"; the latter have neither reward (*śākār;* cf. 4:9) nor legacy (9:5). The deceased are bereft of love, hatred (cf. 3:8; 9:1), and envy (or better "zeal"; cf. 4:4). They have no "share" (*ḥēleq*) in the vain vitality of life (cf. 5:18–19 [Heb. vv. 17–18]).

The sage has come to realize that life, for all its irreconcilable qualities, its tragic absurdities and sustaining moments of joy, its grace and godforsakenness, is to be preferred over death. This blanket affirmation of life marks a significant departure from the sage's earlier preference to the bliss of death (4:2–3; 6:3–6). Faced with the utter vacuousness of death, Qoheleth now casts his lot with the fray of life. Foundational to life is an *élan vital,* a power that manifests itself in bewildering ways yet shares nothing in common with death. By Qoheleth's definition, death is devoid of activity and thought; it is a realm of inert emptiness (9:10). While death is the Vanity that ends all vanities, the absolute zero of all activity, life, however brief, is fraught with effort and activity. Coming to terms with the void enables the living to continue their toil and appropriate joy. Whereas the "fear of the Lord is the beginning of knowledge" for the sages of Proverbs (Prov. 1:7), it is the awareness of life's ephemeral span that marks the beginning of wisdom for Qoheleth, a knowledge that leads to unpretentious reverence and even resilient joy. Such is wisdom from the tomb!

In the stark light of death's "certainty," Qoheleth gives his fullest commendation of enjoyment in what follows (Eccl. 9:7–10). Reaching a greater level of intensity than in his previous reflections, the language of commendation is now cast as command. The series of imperatives adds a sense of urgency to the task of enjoyment: go, eat, drink, let, enjoy, do! In the strongest terms possible, Qoheleth urges his readers to embrace the good in life before it is too late, to seize the day before death seizes the self. As the termination of life is more fully realized, so life's joyful opportunities, its internal possibilities, are set in sharper relief. The darkness only enhances the weak radiance of joy's light, and life's brevity underscores the moral of the moment.

Consonant with his earlier commendations, Qoheleth urges his readers to relish the simple pleasures of eating and drinking (v. 7a), and he provides a distinctly theological rationale: one's deeds have met God's approval (cf. 2:26). What those deeds are, specifically, Qoheleth does not say. Although the rationale is cast in a way that would suggest that God has issued a carte blanche for all human activity, foremost among the divinely sanctioned deeds for the sage are no doubt those that embrace the good, including joy. There is nothing particulary austere or ascetic about Qoheleth's vision of the divinely approved life. Quite the contrary, enjoyment is elevated to a sublime level in the sage's moral sensibility. Joy exhibits both a moral urgency and a palpable beauty: Qoheleth commends wearing fresh, white garments and putting on fragrant oil as signs of joy (see 9:8). The color white connotes festivity as well as purity. Oil conveys joy, fellowship, and sanctity (Pss. 23:5; 133:2; Isa. 61:3). Moreover, the joy of companionship, particularly of marital companionship, is urged in the next command. The admonition is comparable to that of Proverbs 5:15–19, which is designed to (re)kindle the flame of marital

93

passion in the face of extramarital temptations (vv. 20–23). Qoheleth esteems the spouse as the lifelong partner in the journey of joy and work, which together comprise humanity's lot (*ḥēleq;* see also Eccl. 5:19 [Heb. v. 18]). Such enduring companionship is comparably reflected in the primal garden, in which man and woman were created for each other in the bond of mutual intimacy and vocation (Gen. 2:18–25).

Often noted is the striking parallel to Qoheleth's exhortation of joy in the Epic of Gilgamesh (see Introduction). On his heroically misguided quest, Gilgamesh encounters the female tavern owner Šiduri, who offers him sage advice. A synoptic comparison of Šiduri's and Qoheleth's advice is telling:

ŠIDURI **Meissner Tablet**	QOHELETH **Ecclesiastes 9:7–10**
Gilgamesh, whither rovest thou? The life thou pursuest thou shalt not find. When the gods created mankind, Death for mankind they set aside, Life in their own hands retaining. Thou, Gilgamesh, let full be thy belly, Make thou merry by day and by night. Of each day make thou a feast of rejoicing, Day and night dance thou and play! Let thy garments be sparkling fresh, Thy head be washed; bathe thou in water. Pay heed to the little one that holds on to thy hand, Let thy spouse delight in thy bosom! For this is the task of [mankind]! (Pritchard, p. 90)	Go, eat your bread with enjoyment and drink your wine with a merry heart; for God has long ago approved what you do. Let your garments always be white; do not let oil be lacking on your head. Enjoy life with the wife whom you love, all the days of your vain life that are given you under the sun, because that is your portion in life and in your toil at which you toil under the sun. Whatever your hand finds to do, do with your might; for there is no work or thought or knowledge or wisdom in Sheol, to which you are going.

94

It is no coincidence that Šiduri and Qoheleth list essentially the same items of value in identical order, from feasting to family (Seow,

Ecclesiastes, pp. 305–6). But equally noteworthy is the fact that one prominent element featured in Qoheleth's commendation is remarkably absent in the Akkadian tale, namely Qoheleth's commendation of work (vv. 9b–10). For the biblical sage, work is just as integral to joy as it is a part of humanity's limiting lot (see also 2:24a; 3:13a, 22; 5:18 [Heb. v. 17]; 8:15b). Here, finally, Qoheleth provides a decisive clue as to why he includes work within joy's embrace.

Despite the burdensome nature of toil, Qoheleth urges his readers to work for all their worth. "Do it with your might," Qoheleth enjoins (9:10a). Work is not an option; it is an ethical duty. Sisyphus, that tragic character of Greek mythology who was condemned by the gods to roll a boulder up a hill only to see it roll back down into the valley whence it came, is the classical example of meaningless toil. Yet Albert Camus finds in Sisyphus a certain inviolable dignity:

> One sees merely the whole effort of a body straining to raise the huge stone, to roll it and push it up a slope a hundred times over; one sees the face screwed up, the cheek tight against the stone, the shoulder gracing the clay-covered mass, the foot wedging it, the fresh start with arms outstretched, the wholly human security of two earth-clotted hands. (Camus, p. 89)

As Qoheleth has consistently claimed, the value of work is not derived from the gain that one's labors may yield but, rather, is found in the very doing of work, in the challenge of formidable toil. Qoheleth finds inalienable dignity in the strain of toil during one's ephemeral life. Moreover, the sage acknowledges a degree of freedom in the exercise of work (*"whatever* your hand finds to do"). The point is not the kind of work to which one devotes himself or herself but the integrity that is exercised in the very act of toiling. To state the obvious, work is an opportunity that does not avail itself in death. Before the great equalizer, work is revealed to be a privileged duty, the self-satisfying expenditure of power, in short, a blessing. In order for one's labors to be meaningful, sufficient rest is a prerequisite, hence, Qoheleth's stress on the essential rhythm of rest and work, of sustenance and toil. Devoid of work and wisdom, death is the vacuum to which all life is headed. Like joy, work concretely embodies the vitality of life. Slowly and subtly, Qoheleth has turned the toil of work into a celebration of the power of life. Gradually, Qoheleth has stripped the weariness from the toil and transformed burdensome labor into a life-affirming vocation, developed and sustained in relationship to others (4:9). Like Sisyphus, Qoheleth finds a measure of dignity in the very act of toiling. But unlike Sisyphus, Qoheleth's joyful toiler is no lone ranger. Community is essential to meaningful labor (see 4:7–12).

Ecclesiastes 9:11–12

The Hegemony of Chance and Calamity

Qoheleth follows up his "litany" of joy with a brief treatise on the indomitable hegemony of chance (vv. 11–12). Not unrelated to the previous section, this unit fuels the urgency with which Qoheleth commends enjoyment: since no one can know, much less control, what will befall him or her, the time is now to appreciate the good things in life. To underscore this point, the sage begins with a series of "object lessons": the sprinter, the warrior, the wise, and the skillful all have their prizes to win or goals to accomplish—even if they are less than noble!—and yet there is nothing to guarantee success in their respective endeavors, Qoheleth claims. Why? Because chance, rather than aspiration and preparation, will always have the upper hand, behind which lies the inscrutable will of God. Human beings lack control in their lives, except perhaps the possibility of self-control, which Qoheleth urges elsewhere (see 5:1–7 [Heb. 4:17–5:6]). Next to death, the only guarantee in life is that accidents will happen, and no one knows when and whom they will strike.

To be sure, one may increase the odds and heighten the probability of success through discipline and training. Qoheleth does not deny that. Yet the certitude of success is hardly a factor in the equation of life. Disaster can strike at any moment, not only frustrating the accomplishment of highly prized goals but also terminating life itself (9:12). As in the previous verse, Qoheleth revels in pertinent examples in verse 12, but now they are drawn from the savage hunt rather than from human work and aspiration. The hunting metaphor serves to highlight death's untamable nature. The snared bird in Proverbs, for example, serves as an apt metaphor for the fate of the senseless youth (Prov. 7:23; 1:17). But for Qoheleth, no amount of intellectual acuity and moral discernment can deliver one from the snare of death.

Ecclesiastes 9:13–18

Wasted Wisdom

96

As in Ecclesiastes 4:13–16 and 5:13–15 (Heb. vv. 12–14), Qoheleth offers a parable, which he follows up with two proverbs, to illustrate wisdom's limited efficacy. A related vignette is given in 4:13–16, that contrasts a foolish king and a poor but wise youth. This time a poor sage is pitted against a powerful king who is besieging his city (9:13–16). Yet the sage has a failsafe plan to deliver the city from the seemingly invincible grip of the enemy. Contrary to the NRSV, the Hebrew allows for a more hypothetical reading of the results: the poor man *might* have delivered the city had he been taken seriously by its citizens (see Seow, *Ecclesiastes,* p. 310). By virtue of his wisdom, the poor man held the key to the city's deliverance, but it was all for naught, since his plan went unheeded. Stated proverbially in verse 17, the quiet words of the wise warrant more attention than the rantings of a king, particularly among fools. But in a world in which wisdom is no longer recognized for what it is, the wise have no voice and folly becomes the norm. As "[p]rophets are not without honor, except in their hometown" (Mark 6:4), so the sage is a *persona non grata* in the world of the absurd.

This anecdote illustrates both wisdom's potential and its impotency, that is, the potential to overcome brute force—a thoroughly traditional message also stressed in the proverb cited in verse 18 (see also 7:19)—and wisdom's incapacity to resolve anything realistically. One may wonder about the sage's plan to rescue the town from impending defeat. But only Qoheleth knows for sure; his deliberate silence captures the imagination of the reader in seeking creative possibilities to the age-old problems of violence and war. But the actual content of the poor man's advice is irrelevant to Qoheleth's point that tragic failure seems to be wisdom's lot. Wisdom has not the power to marshal the necessary wherewithal to ensure its effectiveness in overcoming daunting odds. Without sufficient social capital, as it were, the exercise of wisdom is all for naught. In a culture of confusion, wisdom leaves scarcely a trace: the wise person remains invisible in a society beset by folly and in a city whose walls are all but breached. The sage has no voice among fools (v. 16b), and wisdom is a lost cause in the hands of a bungling idiot (NRSV "sinner," v. 18). Wisdom, in short, can thrive only in the best of all possible worlds. Qoheleth's world is not one of them.

Ecclesiastes 10:1–20
Miscellaneous Musings

Continuing the theme of the previous section, 10:1 introduces a series of proverbs and prose snippets that cover a wide variety of topics. The first three proverbs explore the contrast between wisdom and folly through various metaphors. The sense of smell described in the first verse graphically illustrates how a modicum of folly overcomes, indeed displaces, a plentitude of wisdom and honor. Folly is likened to the stench of death, while wisdom and honor are compared to the pleasant scent of perfume. But even a slight whiff of foul odor can quickly dispel sweet fragrance. So is folly to wisdom. Would that it be otherwise!

As stench is the antithesis of sweet scent, so the "heart of the wise" and that of the fool are oriented in diametrically opposing ways, both cognitively and morally (v. 2; cf. 7:4). They literally face in opposite directions. Since the heart in Hebrew anthropology denotes the seat of intelligence and will, Qoheleth claims that sagacity and stupidity, the moral and the immoral, are mutually exclusive domains that define the self. The opposite directions of right and left refer not to political leanings, as they can in modern discourse, but to moral bearing. The right connotes goodness and favor in biblical tradition, whereas the left can designate what is wrong and inferior (e.g., Gen. 48:12–20; Matt. 25:31–46). As opposite as these directions are, so folly distinguishes itself categorically from wisdom. There is, moreover, nothing hidden or subtle about folly, for foolishness invariably showcases itself (Eccl. 10:3). Folly leads to aimless drifting, even along a road (v. 15). Lacking direction, fools naturally point to themselves, as in the simple act of walking and declaring themselves—or everyone else (the Hebrew is ambiguous)—as fools.

The next unit, verses 4–6, addresses the issue of royal etiquette. The sage advises any employee of the royal court to maintain a calm composure when subjected to the king's wrath (v. 4). Royal anger must be met head-on, not with guile or fear but with placating calmness, for only by such a response is there any hope of a credible and fair resolution. Qoheleth's advice reflects the sentiment evocatively expressed in Proverbs 25:15: "With patience a ruler may be persuaded, and a soft tongue can break bones" (cf. 16:14). Anger met by anger only ensures needless conflict and destruction from the one who is stronger, the "ruler" in this case (cf. Eccl. 6:10). Through self-assurance and calm comportment, the king's subject does not *escape* accountability but is, rather, prepared to face it, standing firm. Such composure, indeed, is the kind of bearing that Qoheleth advises his readers to assume in a world created by an all-powerful, inscrutable God. Such is the nature of pious "fear" (cf. 3:14; 5:2, 7 [Heb. vv. 1, 6]), a "fearless fear," as it were, as opposed to the terrible dread that inspires either paralysis or defiance.

The next group of verses critically develops the theme of power (Eccl. 10:5–7). Qoheleth, as elsewhere, bears witness to an "evil . . . under the sun" (e.g., 4:1; 5:13; 6:1). The sage attributes this evil to someone who holds the reins of economic power ("ruler") and has upset the status quo: the fool and the rich have traded places, so, too, slaves and princes. The economic world has been turned upside down. The prospect of a world gone mad is not something the sages take lightly (e.g., Prov. 30:21–23; Job 12:17–19; see Van Leeuwen, pp. 599–610).

For others, however, a world on the brink of turbulent change is a source of wonder and testimony to the power of God's "revolutionary" ways. Hannah, for example, testifies to God's incomparable sovereignty, as evinced in the reversals of social status: "The Lord makes poor and makes rich; he brings low, he also exalts. He raises up the poor from the dust; he lifts the needy from the ash heap, to make them sit with princes and inherit a seat of honor" (1 Sam. 2:7–8a; see also Ps. 113:7; Luke 1:52–53). Hannah's testimonial to divine strength suggests the possibility that the "ruler" to whom Qoheleth credits the social reversals described in Ecclesiastes 10:5–7 might be God. Yet, despite the apparent absurdity of such reversals, the sage seems to take pains to *accept* God's inscrutable handiwork, not to criticize it, much less reject it. Perhaps the most that this somber sage can muster is to indict this tumultuous state of affairs as a blunder of divine proportions.

The next grouping of proverbs makes reference to certain kinds of manual labor, along with their accompanying risks, and mines them for their metaphorical value (vv. 8–11). Falling into the pit of one's own digging—a classic case of self-entrapment through malicious scheming or careless conduct—is a popular image in conventional wisdom (Prov. 26:27). Yet no hint of morally dubious behavior is discernable in the following job-related dangers that Qoheleth lists. A stone boundary or fence, which consists of unhewn stones joined without mortar, can provide a secure nest for poisonous snakes, the disturbance of which would not be to anyone's advantage. A person, moreover, can easily be injured in quarrying and demolition work. From pit digging to log splitting, Qoheleth conveys a sample of hazardous occupations in which a little bit of wisdom can prove helpful in ensuring success and minimizing risk. Wisdom, for example, dictates that one's tools be sharp, so as to conserve one's energies in the task at hand. Therein lies wisdom's advantage. Yet, as demonstrated time and again, wisdom also has its limitations; its efficacy is subject to chance and accident like everything else, as much as snake charming is subject to the serpent's will (v. 11; see also 9:11–12). Wisdom is thus no panacea. Indeed, there are many occasions in which wisdom serves only to generate false hope, particularly with regard to profitable gain, until reality "bites back."

99

From occupational hazards, Qoheleth turns his attention to the dangers of discourse in verses 12–14. There are self-edifying words, as conveyed by the wise, and there is self-destructive discourse, as uttered by fools. As the idleness of fools is self-consuming, so also is their discourse (4:6). Foolish discourse, benign as it may seem, only perpetuates "wicked madness." Such maleficent nonsense, Qoheleth implies, is bound up with certain presumptions about what the future might hold (10:14b). Yet, as Qoheleth repeatedly contends, the future is impenetrably shrouded from human perception, a frequent theme in Qoheleth's thought (e.g., 3:11; 6:12b; 7:14b). The unpredictability of the future undercuts all forms of prognostication, whether they emerge from an optimistic reliance upon the continuance of things or result in dramatic predictions of radical transformation, as found in prophetic and apocalyptic visions, veritable "dreams" in Qoheleth's eyes (5:3, 7 [Heb. vv. 2, 6]). Such efforts are not only a waste of time and effort, they are dangerous, for they lead to false hopes and plans. Better to focus on the present rather than toil like fools for the future. Such toil bespeaks pathetic disorientation: "[Fools] do not even know the way to town" (10:15 cf. v. 3).

The last section of this chapter is associated with the proper form of royal practice, ending with an exhortation to respect the king (vv. 16–20). The first two verses convey two contrasting scenarios. Together, they illustrate the tie that binds the land's welfare with the integrity of royal office. The land flourishes when the king is of noble stock and stature, but it suffers when he is a mere servant (more accurately, "youth," *na'ar;* but cf. 4:13–16). The unorthodox background of the king reflects unorthodox behavior in the royal court: the princes put on their lavish banquets in the morning, and the day of sober rule is ruined.

There is a proper time for "feasting," Qoheleth admits, but it is not at the crack of dawn. Untimely feasting constitutes carousing and reflects a flagrant disregard for the propriety accorded the political office. The proper context and purpose for feasting is "strength" (v. 17b), a term associated with intellectual and moral power in addition to physical prowess. To be sure, feasting has its edifying place in the royal rhythm of governance, as the simple act of eating does elsewhere for Qoheleth in daily life. Feasting leads to joy, and that is no insignificant matter for Qoheleth (v. 19), but if it is conducted in excess, thereby leading to indolence, then the unrepaired roof will eventually collapse on the revelers (v. 18)! As the queen mother in Proverbs advises her son, King Lemuel, "it is not for kings to drink wine, or for rulers to desire strong drink; or else they will drink and forget what has been decreed, and will pervert the rights of all the afflicted" (Prov. 31:4–5). In the "strength" that is gained only through maturity and prudence, the powers-that-be know when to feast and when to stop for the sake of the land and its inhabitants (Eccl. 5:9 [Heb. v. 8]).

The final verse in chapter 10, however, lends a note of fearful circumspection to the sage's political commentary. Prudence dictates that one's mouth be vigilantly guarded, lest a curse escape from one's lips and be reported (v. 20). As Seow points out, the aviary figures in this verse may allude to the ubiquitous presence of royal spies or informants in the land (*Ecclesiastes*, p. 341). In any case, whether as friend or fowl, an informant can gain access to one's subversive thoughts even within the most private of settings. As the sage identified certain occupational hazards elsewhere (see 10:8–11), so Qoheleth acknowledges a prominent danger in cursing the king. Circumspection of one's potentially inflammatory thoughts coheres well with the common sapiential sentiment that the tongue requires continual restraint (e.g., 5:6 [Heb. v. 5]; Prov. 10:19, 32; 11:12; 12:18; 15:1; 17:28). Given the king's unmatched power and range of "hearing," it is best not to be in the public or private business of political critique, even if the sage himself, not to mention his predecessors, has occasionally (and discreetly) attempted it (Eccl. 4:13–16; 5:8–9 [Heb. vv. 7–8]; Prov. 28:15–16; 29:4, 12, 26).

Ecclesiastes 11:1–6
The Resourcefulness of Giving

The following six verses can be grouped together in terms of their common theme: the advisability of distributing one's charitable lot in the face of future uncertainty. Scholars, however, are divided regarding the precise significance of the first two verses. The first verse, in particular, has been read in various ways, some suggesting that the sage is encouraging investment in maritime trade (so Longman, p. 256), while others take the verse as exhorting charity (so Seow, *Ecclesiastes*, pp. 341–44). The latter sense seems more in line with apparent Near Eastern parallels, as well as with the history of interpretation. Compare, for example, the Egyptian proverb "Do a good deed and throw it in the water; when it dries you will find it" from *Instruction of Ankhsheshonq* (Lichtheim, p. 174) and the Arabic proverb "Do good, throw your bread on the waters, and one day you will find it."

If this proverb were meant to encourage investment in maritime trade, the rationale in verse 1b would not provide much of an incentive:

one expects *more* than simply receiving one's investment after some time (and waterlogged at that!). No return on the return, a zero percent yield, is no inducement. Qoheleth is likely referring to the good deed given freely. As it stands, the proverb contends that in the act of giving, something is inevitably given back. Indeed, one can expect it, although the "return" may not be immediate. One can find a similar point made in Proverbs: "Whoever is kind to the poor lends to the LORD, and will be repaid in full" (Prov. 19:17). In both proverbs, the claim is that what is given does not dissipate or vanish, as one might expect in casting a morsel of bread into a vast ocean of need. Rather, one good deed deserves another.

To be sure, it appears uncharacteristically optimistic for Qoheleth to contend that something beneficial awaits the giver, that charity leads to mutual benefit, much in contrast to the modern cynical proverb "No good deed goes unpunished." Nevertheless, the reference to "bread" in 11:1 connotes elsewhere for the sage the means of sustenance and joy, an eminently positive theme for the sage, particularly in his various commendations: for example, "Go, eat your bread with enjoyment" (9:7; see also 5:18; 8:15 [Heb. v. 17]; but cf. 9:11b). In context, 11:1 suggests that part of the pleasure of life is found not only in receiving sustenance but also in offering it to others. By sharing sustenance, one will invariably receive the same treatment, the same gifts. Hospitality breeds hospitality. Both modern and ancient etiquette dictate that a dinner invitation be repaid with another among friends. Jesus, however, exposes such hospitality as self-serving, reflecting an etiquette of elitism in light of the ethos of God's kingdom in Luke 14:12–14. One must, however, keep in mind that Qoheleth is interested not so much in the social graces as, more broadly, in the intersection of ethics and joy. It is fitting that joy be shared in fellowship. Charity, in short, is an investment in joy, no more, no less. "Repayment" is the reciprocity the good deed engenders.

In Barbara Kingsolver's novel *Animal Dreams,* a young horticulturist named Hallie has gone off to Nicaragua to aid the peasants. In a letter to her sister Codi back in the States, she explains her reasons:

> Wars and elections are both too big and too small to matter in the long run. The daily work—that goes on, it adds up. It goes into the ground, into crops, into children's bellies and their bright eyes. Good things don't get lost (Kingsolver, p. 299).

"Good things don't get lost" is precisely Qoheleth's point.

The first verse is, no doubt, to be read with the second, which seems to advocate a prudent course of financial planning in the face of possible impending disaster (so NRSV). However, the Hebrew literally reads: "Give a portion to seven, or even eight." In other words, Qoheleth is concerned with diversifying not so much one's assets as one's stewardship! The numerical values in themselves are not significant. The point is that a portion of one's income should not be devoted to any one cause or recipient alone, an altruistic twist on the modern proverb, "Don't put all your eggs in one basket." By diversifying one's giving, charity is shared more equitably within the larger community, and the initial giver is bound to be a recipient in this new, widening network of care. Pragmatist that he is, Qoheleth roots such charity in terms of self-preservation.

The following verses elaborate on the limitations of human knowledge (vv. 3–6). Even though one can count on the clouds to bring rain and trees to fall eventually to the ground, one does not know when the rain will come or precisely where a tree will fall. Obsessive weather watching will not guarantee a productive yield; indeed, to the contrary, it can paralyze all agricultural efforts, from sowing to reaping (v. 4). Agriculture, as with any kind of vocational activity, carries with it certain inherent risks. Nature is essentially free from human manipulation: no one can literally "guard the wind" (v. 4; see 8:8), much less "chase after" it (e.g., 1:17; 2:26; 4:16; 6:9). Moreover, just as the wind's directions in the heavens cannot be predicted (cf. 1:6), so one cannot determine how the wind or "life-breath" (*rûaḥ*) confers life to the fetus (v. 5). The wind's course and the mystery of birth remain free of human contrivance, Qoheleth avers. They serve as metonyms for the mystery of creation. Yet one has no choice except to continue working as one can (cf. 9:10), sowing seed in the morning and keeping active in the evening, unperturbed by the vicissitudes of the world. Diligence and diversification of labor, in contrast to all-consuming obsession (cf. 4:8), are the keys to relative security, for one never knows which enterprise will in time prove advantageous. Given humanity's inability to foresee the future (another mark of "vanity"), diversifying one's efforts is the only prudent thing to do.

Ecclesiastes 11:7—12:8
The Agony and Ecstasy of Vanity: Joy and Death

Followed by an epilogue (12:9–14), this major unit concludes Qoheleth's discourse. As the sage began his ruminations with a vision of cosmic weariness and monotony (1:2–11), so he ends on a note that is

103

no less encompassing: the demise of life (12:2–7). Since Qoheleth prefers the "end of a thing" over its beginning (7:4), the conclusion of his discourse discloses something of the purpose and scope of his work as a whole. Ecclesiastes is essentially an obituary of life itself (see Introduction). But the way by which Qoheleth gets to his conclusion is just as important as his destination. As noted in Qoheleth's cosmic preface, there is a fluid movement between cosmos and corpus, between cosmology and anthropology. Creation, like humanity's lot, is marked by relentless toil, but all in all accomplishing nothing. Qoheleth's world is a reflection of his vain life, indeed of the life of any mortal, and the denouement is no exception.

The Gravity of Joy (11:7–10)

Qoheleth takes the issue of joy with dead seriousness. As creation began with light separating the darkness, so Qoheleth begins his final observations with the delight of light to the eyes (11:7). "To see the sun" is to bask in the warmth and joy that life offers (cf. 6:5; 7:11). Such is joy's foundation, the vitality of life. But it cannot last, for the "days of darkness" will inevitably arrive. Yet that, too, paradoxically, is cause for joy, according to the sage. Knowing that the prime of one's life, along with its accompanying blessings of health and prosperity, is fleeting only underscores the import of joy. There are those who eat in darkness full of resentment, for they have toiled endlessly, denying themselves, with nothing to show for it (4:7–8; 5:17 [Heb. v. 16]). They have sacrificed the opportunity for joy upon the altar of elusive gain. But then there are those who, because they neither took for granted nor denied themselves the blessings of life's serendipities, can face their impending days of darkness with acceptance and even contentment. Such is the key to human existence for the sage: to relinquish control over life in order to be freed for joy.

The reference to the youth in 11:9 fits well into Qoheleth's commendation, for it evokes the vital capacity to exhaust the joyous moment for all its edifying worth (see 6:4; 7:14; 9:11–12). In this verse, Qoheleth's thought is crystalized in direct discourse. Addressing the "young man," a cipher for the reader, the sage extols joy: "Follow the inclination of your heart and the desire of your eyes" (cf. 2:10). Compared to traditional wisdom, such sage advice appears particularly ill advised. The parental sage of Proverbs, for example, urges his son to walk blamelessly and fear the LORD, rather than to "rejoice in doing evil and delight in the perverseness of evil" (Prov. 2:14). The teacher in Proverbs views the impulsive joy of youth with a weary eye, associating it with immoral conduct. Furthermore, in the Babylonian *Epic of Gilgamesh* the elders warn the protagonist who seeks a life of boundless accomplishment: "You are young, Gilgamesh, your heart carries you off" (see Introduction). Discipline and caution, by contrast, are the conventional virtues of the promising youth. Such wisdom is pedagogically aimed at inculcating in the youth a *submissive* heart as the basis of virtue. By comparison, it would appear that Qoheleth is cultivating youthful *waywardness* rather than instilling right character. The Codex Vaticanus translation of Ecclesiastes 11:9aγ mitigates, if not contravenes, the thrust of Qoheleth's advice as conveyed in the Hebrew: "Follow the inclination of your heart *blamelessly* (Greek *amōmos*), but *not* the desire of your eyes"! The translator qualifies Qoheleth's advice to the point of contradicting it. Indeed, Qoheleth seems to contradict Mosaic law, posing a vexing problem for the early rabbis:

> You will remember all the commandments of the LORD and do them, and *not follow the lust of your own heart and your own eyes.* (Num. 15:39; italics added)

There is, however, an aspect of traditional wisdom that is consonant with Qoheleth's ostensibly unprecedented advice, namely, that of joy, modeled after wisdom before her creator (Prov. 8:31) and embodied by the student in her home (9:5). Qoheleth exhorts the youth— equivalent to the listening son in Proverbs—to cultivate and exercise that joy with all his heart, soul, and might, as it were. Anxiety and pain (but not sorrow!) are the antitheses of joy, for they are the bitter accompaniments of obsessive "striving" (see 4:7–8; 5:13–17 [Heb. vv. 12–16]). Nothing is to be gained from them (see Matt. 6:25–34; Luke 12:22–34). Rather, accompanying the joy that Qoheleth commends is the sure knowledge that God will judge one's conduct (Eccl. 11:9b). But this theme of judgment is designed not to *temper* Qoheleth's command to enjoy life but to *underscore* and *direct* it. "For Koheleth, the enjoyment of life becomes the highest dictate of life" (Gordis, p. 335; so also Towner, p. 353). Whereas the NRSV translates the final clause in verse 9 as adversative ("but . . ."), it is better treated as a simple conjunction and even left untranslated as part of this catenation of commands: "Rejoice . . . , let . . . , follow . . . , (and) know that for all these things God will bring you into judgment." Divine judgment is not a corrective but an incentive, the very foundation of the sage's command to enjoy. As Qoheleth notes elsewhere, enjoyment is a gift of God (2:24–26; 3:12–13; 5:18–20 [Heb. vv. 17–19]; 9:7, 9).

Terse and direct, the sage's advice unfortunately does not give any particulars that would flesh out his vision of youth. What is clear,

105

however, is that Qoheleth is safeguarding a stage of life from being crushed by excessive responsibilities and their accompanying worries ("anxiety" and "pain"). In so doing, the sage not only warns the youth (literally "young man"), his expressed audience, but also critiques his culture at large. Youth, Qoheleth contends, is that liminal stage in the maturation process that must be carefully nurtured and protected. It is the preface to full adulthood that must remain exempt, however fleetingly, from self-restraining responsibilities and concerns. There is, moreover, a freedom that avails itself only to youth that should be enjoyed without being exploited. Whereas conventional wisdom consistently casts a weary eye toward the vagaries of youth, seeking to rein in youth's impetuosity, Qoheleth provides a refreshingly positive view. While the "son" in Proverbs 1—9 remains silent and submissive, the "young man" in Ecclesiastes is exhorted to exert himself in joy. Qoheleth the old sage, much like a typical grandparent, provides the necessary balance to the harsh admonitions of the parental voice in Proverbs. The combined effect is the formative education of youth.

The ancient sage offers a vision of youthful joy that is at root salutary; however, it is not one that revels in the kind of self-abandonment that leads to self-destruction or harm. Qoheleth by no means endorses the carefree life of self-gratification. Such a reckless pleasure rests on the illusion of immortality, a misconception the sage vigorously corrects in his final words (11:10b—12:7), as he does earlier (see discussion of 9:3). For Qoheleth, the illusion of immortality is in fact the root of all misery. On the one hand, the ancient sage is far from encouraging a lifestyle that would only hasten one's death, not to mention harm others. Such would be pure folly (see 7:17). On the other hand, a lifestyle characterized by austere and ascetic displays of righteousness, a masochistic way of life that indulges in either self-flagellation or obsessive striving, proves more deleterious than salutary (7:16). And that is precisely the point in the sage's address to the youth. Qoheleth contends that there is a self-edifying prudence that does not stifle youthful exuberance yet does set constructive boundaries in the exercise of joy. Youth marks the height of a person's physical capacity and enchantment with life as well as the pinnacle of joy and freedom, a liberation from the angst of striving that only gives rise to discontentment in later adulthood. Such a lesson, in fact, is directed not simply to youths proper but to all readers.

As the "son" in Proverbs 1—9 represents the silent subject of the reader, the "youth" in Qoheleth's discourse designates not only a certain age category but also the reader at large. Ever more fleeting in old age, the simple gifts of joy still avail themselves, from the delights of

106

taste to the joy of companionship. Indeed, their import is only heightened as one's age progresses. Qoheleth encourages the youth to cultivate such joys with exuberance. For the mature of heart, such joyful fervor can even teach an old "living dog" some new tricks (see 9:4). On the one hand, to become exclusively duty-bound and striving, Qoheleth warns, is to violate an essential part of human living and, thereby, to nurture only worry and resentment. On the other hand, to hold desperately on to youth as if it were an eternal fetish is tantamount to struggling against death's sure victory (see below). Life is not a conquest. For the sage, the full exercise of joy enables one to age graciously, to accept without resentment all that life offers, both good and bad. In short, the vitality of youth must not be taken for granted. Neither should youth's earnest passions be denounced. Qoheleth is dead serious about youth's all-too fleeting virtues. Youth represents the robust embodiment of *carpe diem,* of seizing with all the vigor of one's being the God-sent moment. But such an ideal, of course, need not be confined to the young.

Qoheleth specifically advises the young person to remove all obstacles that would prevent him or her from taking on those life-affirming adventures that naturally fall within youth's domain. If such occasions for joy are avoided in the name of duty or shunned because of angst or self-righteous denial, they will no doubt be counted as opportunities forever lost in later life. Qoheleth's call to joy is, thus, an urgent one for young and old alike. Qoheleth's exhortation is the closest the sage ever gets to a divine imperative. His peculiar ethos of joy rests upon two fundamental assumptions: the "vanity" or brevity of youth (v. 10) and the prospect of divine accountability (v. 9b). Together, death and judgment motivate and shape the youth's appropriation of joy, the kind of enjoyment that nurtures rather than suppresses the vitality of life. By invoking both, Qoheleth has transformed his final, seventh call to joy into a sapiential *shema,* his greatest commandment (cf. Deut. 6:4). The appropriation of joy marks nothing less than a moral triumph.

The Gravity of Death (12:1–8)

Following on the heels of his call to affirm the irrepressible joys of youth, Qoheleth concludes his reflections on a somber note, to put it mildly. As Qoheleth's reflections opened with "creation," so they end with death, described in a series of evocative and enigmatic images. Whereas the previous section (11:7–10) stressed the primacy of the present, the following verses attend to the demise of the future. Given Qoheleth's outlook on life's vanity, the latter flows naturally from the

107

former, the void from the vitality. For the sage, to live fully does not mean holding out for the future. One can never be sure whether the future holds something better than what the present moment offers. But there is one thing about the future that is incontrovertible, death. As the certain reality of death provides the point of departure for Qoheleth's call to joy in 11:7–10, it concludes his quest for meaning in 12:1–8. Death exposes all illusions of grandeur and ultimate gain. It purges the soul of all futile striving and, paradoxically, anxiety. Qoheleth's discourse ends on a remarkably cathartic note with the person's life-breath returning to God (12:7). The eternal sleep of death serves as a wake-up call to live and welcome the serendipities of the present.

Interpreters, both ancient and modern, have taken 12:1–8 in various ways as a description of the aging body, a crumbling house, an approaching thunderstorm, a passing funeral, or some combination thereof. Most recently, Seow has argued that Qoheleth's final words depict nothing short of the eschatological destruction of the cosmos (Seow, "Qoheleth's Eschatological Poem," pp. 209–34). The problem, however, with each interpretation is the strained attempt to limit the poem's connotations primarily to a single setting. On the one hand, the poem foils any strict allegorical reading by which the literal images are meant to be discarded for some hidden constellation of meanings (Fox, "Aging and Death in Qohelet 12," pp. 59–71). It is impossible to discern, for example, a point-by-point correspondence between every image in the poem and some aspect of the aging body. On the other hand, the images presented by Qoheleth are fraught with background. The distinct lack of consistency among the various images defies any attempt at establishing some univocal setting, be it cosmic or individual, funerary or domestic (see also Murphy, pp. 115–16).

The remarkably diverse settings conveyed in this concluding section are designed to convey both the terror and inevitability of death in all arenas of life. In rapid succession, Qoheleth hops from cosmos to corpus, from household to funeral setting, accompanied by numerous symbolic images that remain shrouded in mystery. The following outline illustrates the movement:

I. Demise of the Cosmos   verse 2
  a. Cosmic darkness
  b. Clouds
II. Demise of the Domicile   verse 3
  a. Incapacitated male "guardians"
  b. Diminished female "grinders"
  c. Dimmed female "onlookers"

III. Demise of Commerce   verse 4a
  a. End of commercial traffic
  b. Decline of the mill sound
IV. The Rise and Demise of the Natural Realm   verse 4b–5a
  a. "Rise" of bird songs
  b. Terror everywhere
  c. Decay and impotence
V. Demise of the Individual   verse 5b–7
  a. Entrance into the "eternal home"
  b. Broken symbols of life
  c. Return to life's genesis

The various settings of life, from the individual to the cosmic, are covered in this ode to death. Yet an underlying focus is sustained throughout, as will be seen, namely, the inexorable demise of human life, both individual and corporate. The cosmic and natural settings conveyed in the poetry serve to underscore Qoheleth's anthropocentric focus, similar to what is found in Job's self-curse in chapter 3. Job's malediction is aimed not only at overturning his birth but also at reversing all of creation. Job 3:3–9 moves back and forth between self-imprecation (vv. 3, 10) and cosmic curse (vv. 4–9). Here, too, corpus meets cosmos. Yet, throughout his deliberations, Job perceives the universe to revolve around him alone. The destruction of the cosmos that Job invokes is meant to ensure his own demise. Job regards the universe as his personal world, a perspective that is decisively undercut by God's response in chapters 38—41.

For Qoheleth, the cosmic purview featured in the sage's final words—even if they are eschatological in scope—serves to underscore the harsh reality of the individual's death, in which the very modes of perceiving the world, including consciousness itself, are extinguished. Put simply, the death of each individual bears cosmic and corporate significance. Moreover, the prospect of eventual cosmic convulsion in and of itself is no incentive for an untroubled youth, whom Qoheleth continues to address in this passage. But an individual's world fraught with joy and vanity, rays of delight and clouds of gloom, is another matter altogether. As the height of one's prowess, both physical and moral, is celebrated under the dazzling light of the sun, so the debilitating onset of old age and death is matched by the darkening of the cosmos. It is this kind of figurative association, rather than allegorical correlation, between the individual and the cosmos that must be kept in mind in order to understand the sage's final words.

Continuing the direct address of 11:9, Qoheleth commands the youth to keep in mind the creator of life in the prime of one's life (12:1),

109

for inseparably tied to knowledge of God is the concomitant awareness of life's finitude and demise. The "days of trouble" correspond to the "days of darkness" indicated in 11:8. They mark death's advent. In the misery that precedes death, the capacity for enjoyment becomes lost (12:1b). As the light of life was beheld by the eyes (11:7), so now it is vanishing. Darkness prevails (12:2). Whereas the sun would be expected to shine "after" the rain, only ominous clouds follow (v. 2b). The sun's life-giving rays are no longer evident.

Not simply a matter of physical decline, death's advent is described in terms of incapacitating terror in verse 3. This verse, above all others, is commonly read as an allegory that depicts the physical ravages of old age: the "women who grind" are the molars; "those who look through windows" indicate the eyes or pupils; and the strong men and guardians presumably refer to the individual's limbs and back, although precise identification is less clear. Such an interpretation is possible, but it glosses over the setting in which this allegedly original allegory is placed. The scene is a picture of domesticity, specifically of a household under attack.

The "guards of the house" and the "strong men" or "men of valor," along with the women who grind grain for bread and peer through windows, presuppose an affluent domestic setting that recalls wisdom's natural domicile and the related household of the "woman of valor" in Proverbs. In Proverbs 9:1–6, wisdom is said to have built her house, prepared a lavish meal of "bread" and "wine," and sent out servant girls to invite her would-be disciples. In 31:10–31, the industrious "woman of valor" (NRSV "capable wife") manages and protects her household from the outside elements (v. 21). More than simply capable, she is a domestic warrior who "girds herself with strength and makes her arms strong," ever defiant of future danger (vv. 17, 25b). As wisdom "incarnated" within the patriarchal household of ancient Israel, this female figure exercises a militant domesticity; her house is a veritable fortress.

As valorous protectors of the household, the men to which Qoheleth refers in Ecclesiastes 12:3 are the male counterparts to the valiant woman of Proverbs 31:10–21. They are guardians of the household as much as the "woman of valor" is the backbone of the home. More than weakened by old age, they cower (NRSV "are bent") in fear before some undisclosed terror. Complementing the demise of male strength is the dwindling number of women who grind flour, an essential household task (Exod. 11:5; Job 31:10; Isa. 47:2). The reference to women looking out through windows recalls a typical scene in biblical

110

narrative: Sisera's mother looks in vain for the return of her son (Judg. 5:28); Michal looks out to see David dancing "promiscuously" before the Ark (2 Sam. 6:16–23); and Jezebel looks through her window to behold her executioner (2 Kings 9:30). But perhaps most telling with respect to Qoheleth's reference to female onlookers is the figure of the wise mother who looks out the "window of [her] house" to behold a senseless young man on the street seduced by a stranger (Prov. 7:7–8). In both scenes, darkness and doom have fallen. The darkening of the heavens is matched by the dimness of sight, a blindness that not even the light of wisdom can overcome.

Drawing from the conventional setting of wisdom's household, Qoheleth graphically illustrates the impotency of wisdom before the inevitability of death. The crumbling domicile was once the thriving house of life, much in contrast to the eternal house of death (Eccl. 12:5). Even the house of the wise cannot stand before death's merciless onslaught, which provokes terror and incapacity even among the most stout of heart. According to conventional wisdom, the wise reside as guests in wisdom's domicile, nourished and edified in this house of life (Prov. 9:1–6; cf. Eccl. 7:2, 4). But now this residence can no longer provide protection. Wisdom, in fact, is nowhere to be found in her house, populated by valorous men and industrious women. Perhaps she has fled, remaining "far off," having vacated her domicile long ago (see 7:24). In short, the sage identifies the one irresolvable crisis that every person must face but for which wisdom, the "tree of life" (Prov. 3:18), can offer no help. No one can escape the yawning maw of death (see Eccl. 8:8). Death's advent is marked by the incapacitation of its victims, destroying both body and mind, strength and perception. Death is the final, ever victorious enemy, against which even wisdom can marshal no defense.

In short, the household setting that permeates 12:3 is intimately tied to wisdom's traditional setting and ethos. By depicting its destruction, Qoheleth has cut to the heart of wisdom's inefficacy before death's destructive appetite. Qoheleth has undermined the life-giving potency that is traditionally associated with wisdom and righteousness, a sapiential power that allegedly preserves one from the "snares of death" (e.g., Prov. 13:14; see also 10:2; 11:4; 12:28). Wisdom's lively household has become an empty shell, a virtual household of death (Eccl. 12:5; cf. 7:2, 4).

Qoheleth's ode to death moves from the domestic setting to the public arena (v. 4). The cessation of all commercial activity is marked by the closing of the double doors of the bazaar (NRSV "street"; *šûq* [so Seow, *Ecclesiastes*, pp. 356–57]). The familiar sound of the mill, in turn, falls to an inaudible level. The grim scene marks the collapse of the marketplace. Given his harsh critique of the self-absorbed economic realities of his day (see Introduction), the demise of the marketplace is of particular significance for Qoheleth, signifying nothing less than the desolation of society as he knows it. The sound of wild birds rises over the silenced din, as all commercial intercourse comes to a grinding halt and the "daughters of song" are brought low, literally "prostrated." This graphic depiction further underscores the futile pursuit of gain for the individual, whose fate is sealed by death.

The identity of these "daughters" is a matter of dispute. Are they professional mourners (so Fox, "Aging and Death in Qoheleth 12," p. 62), or "birds" swooping low to spy out possible prey, as might be suggested by the poetic parallel in the previous clause (so Seow, *Ecclesiastes,* p. 360)? Both interpretations, however, have their problems. Throughout biblical literature, "song" (*šîr*) is never associated with mourning or lament (*qînâ;* cf. Jer. 9:17–19; 2 Chron. 35:25). The funeral setting is not assumed until verse 5b (contra Fox). Against Seow's ornithological reading of verse 4b, the form of the verb is passive: something has *forced* the "daughters of song" low, in effect humbling or incapacitating them. (The alleged verbal parallel Seow cites from Job 38:40, of the lion "crouching" for his prey, takes the active form.) Regardless of their identity, the "daughters of song," like the "grinders" in the previous verse," are female and, thus, most likely refer to female singers of some sort (see Exod. 15:21 [Miriam]; Judg. 5:1 [Deborah]; 2 Sam. 19:36; Ezra 2:65; Neh. 7:67 ["female singers"]). Perhaps the "singers" and the "grinders" overlap in identity. In Jeremiah 25:10, the "sound of joy" and the "sound of millstones" are associated. In any case, while the song of the bird rises, singing women are brought low, signifying the collapse of community in all its varied activities.

Just as the men of strength are brought to their knees, bent and trembling (v. 3), so women of song are forced to the ground. The source of their debilitation is found in the following verse: terror "from on high" (NRSV "heights") and "in the road" (v. 5). Qoheleth is probably not describing the fear of heights that accompanies the feebleness of old age, as is often suggested. Rather, he depicts the onset of approaching terror that incapacitates men and women, whether in the home or on the street. From above and below, this dreadful entity encroaches upon the living, lurching ever closer and wreaking destruction in its path. Its name is death, whose "picture cannot be drawn," as the ancient sage Utanapishtim declares to Gilgamesh (see Introduction). Qoheleth, too, vividly paints the ravages of this imageless enemy.

The incapacitation and destruction of human beings is also reflected in the natural, specifically botanical, realm. The almond tree, the locust (NRSV "grasshopper," *ḥāgāb*), and the caperberry (NRSV "desire") all give evidence of nature's languishing. Not coincidentally, they also symbolize the feebleness of old age. The blooming of the almond tree could represent graying hair and at the same time convey a sense of repulsiveness, given the unique form of the verb in Hebrew (Seow, *Ecclesiastes*, pp. 361–62). The drooping locust (more likely the plant than the insect!) and the failed caperberry—considered an aphrodisiac in ancient times—suggest the onset of infirmity and impotence. On the surface, this verse limns the blight of vegetation, which would signal the general desolation of nature. Yet given the particular choice of plants, another level of significance is suggested that falls squarely within the human domain. Human life is destined to insidious deterioration, and age, rather than an object of respect, is turned into an object of revulsion (cf. Prov. 16:31; 20:29).

The stage is now set for the human self to pass through the threshold of death's domain ("eternal house"), as the mourners process through the public streets (v. 5b). All that has been described heretofore, from the darkening of the cosmos to the cessation of commerce, points to the individual's passage into the realm of the dead. The life of the human being, from corporate to personal, is dismantled in all aspects. With death having claimed the individual, the funeral setting comes to the fore and extends through verse 6. Certain symbols of life—from the snapped "silver cord" to the smashed jar—are broken or destroyed, perhaps reflecting certain elements of an ancient funeral rite (see Seow, *Ecclesiastes*, p. 381). This final setting also marks the conclusion of a much larger movement, namely, that of human life from its native domicile (v. 3)—the salutary house built by wisdom—to the house of death, which personified folly traditionally inhabits (Prov. 9:13–18). Death, in Enkidu's words, is the "house of Darkness . . . where those who enter do not come out, . . . where dirt is their drink, their food is of clay" (see Introduction). Such is the height of "vanity" (Eccl. 12:8). Through a parade of various images and settings in life, from the cosmic to the familial, Qoheleth depicts the harrowing journey toward death. Considered the archetypal enemy, death inspires paralyzing fear; its victory is assured for each and every human being (cf. 8:8).

Yet it need not be so. For all the ravages that fall upon the human being, the poem concludes on a relatively cathartic note in 12:7: the brutality of death leads to the natural return of the body ("dust") to the earth and of the breath (*rûaḥ*) to the Creator, whence it came. As in

113

1:4, the earth remains the same, receiving back what was taken from it to create life. The earth does not dissolve away. Qoheleth's ode to death does not so much revel in the eschatological travails of cosmic destruction—although such hyperbole is employed—as document the natural outcome of life for each and every individual. Recalling the primal garden story, this final verse in the poem poignantly depicts the natural outcome of life, the return of an individual's life to its genesis as a necessary part of life (Gen. 2:7; 3:19). A generation goes but another comes (Eccl. 1:4). For Qoheleth, the death of the individual bears cosmic significance.

By presenting death in all its gravity, the ancient sage seeks to impart a new outlook on life to the addressed youth and, by extension, to the reader. Even death bears some pedagogical value. The method behind the madness of death is not unlike that found in Charles Dickens's novella *A Christmas Carol.* In the tale, Ebenezer Scrooge meets the "Ghost of Christmas Yet to Come," the culminating scene in Scrooge's conversion, and through it comes face to face with his own miserable death. The outcome of his encounter is a converted life filled with charity and joy for the Scrooge of the present. Banishing all anxiety and miserliness, Scrooge is no longer the misanthrope that he was. The terrifying prospect of a lonely and loveless death becomes both his undoing and his reconstitution.

With similar effect, Qoheleth underscores the misery of death in order to instruct the "youth" and the reader to live life to the fullest (11:9). By vividly conveying the totalizing terror of death, the sage counters the youth's temptation to think of himself or herself as immortal. The language of the psalmist's petition is strikingly similar: "The terrors of death have fallen upon me./Fear and trembling come upon me, and horror overwhelms me" (Ps. 55:4b–5). Yet amid the histrionics of human resistance and fear, Qoheleth subtly offers another way of confronting death. Death need not be the violent enemy whose fearsome power can paralyze the living. Qoheleth has found a way to take the sting out of death, and it begins by *accepting* death's victory and living accordingly (Eccl. 8:8; cf. 1 Cor. 15:55).

Qoheleth's commendations of joy, as in 11:9, are ultimately founded upon the necessity of accepting death as a natural part of life. By coming to terms with death, an individual can "seize the day" (*carpe diem*) while it lasts before the days of darkness come and seize the self! This message is most paradoxically stated in two proverbs, no doubt with Qoheleth's stamp of approval, if not from his own hand:

114

It is better to go to the house of mourning
than to go to the house of feasting;

for this is the end of everyone,
  and the living will lay it to heart.
                    (7:2)

The heart of the wise is in the house of mourning;
  but the heart of fools is in the house of mirth.
                    (7:4)

As in the poem about death, the use of the domestic setting ("house") is telling. As noted above (see 7:1–14), Qoheleth urges the wise to inhabit the house of mourning, where the prospect of death is squarely faced, and to avoid the "house of rejoicing," the domicile of denial inhabited by fools. As in 12:3 and 5b, Qoheleth reverses the traditional understanding of wisdom's domestic and salutary nature. The wise know how to accept death, for it is only through mourning that true joy can be found (7:3b). In the house of mourning, death is accepted by the living. In his final poem, the sage exposes the house of the strong as a house of futility, whose inhabitants valiantly try to fend off death's onslaughts but to no avail. Yet the wise, who have learned to live fully in the days of fortune and to accept their lot in the days of adversity (7:14), are equipped to face death without fear and resentment (cf. 5:17). Ecclesiastes is not so much a tomb as a hospice in which the dying teach the living.

As the wise have led their lives in resourceful contentment, receiving the joy and enjoying their work, so they accept their death, content with the brevity of their life. Like joy, death, too, is a serendipity to be received; it is not a matter of retribution. Like the rain that falls on the just and the unjust (Matt. 5:45), so death comes to all. In association with the "cosmic" theme of economic gain raised in the opening of the book (1:3), Qoheleth concludes that the struggle *for* such gain is, at root, a struggle *against* death, a losing battle if there ever was one (see 1:3; 2:11, 14–23; 3:9; 5:16 [Heb. v. 15]). As with Gilgamesh, the struggle against death, no matter how heroic, amounts to nothing. Death conquers all. It is the final "master" that devours the fruits of one's livelihood, the quintessential stranger that inspires fear and loathing (cf. 2:19; 6:2). No amount of wisdom or human strength will thwart death's insatiable appetite. *True* wisdom, rather, lies in the living of *these* days, before the sickle cuts its wide swath. In this poetic finale, Qoheleth limns the vanity of humanity's plight before death and in so doing demonstrates joy's prudence, the source of humanity's redemption.

With death as the outcome of life, "all is vanity" (12:8). So Qoheleth (or his editor) concludes as he began his ruminations, namely, with his

115

verdict on all existence (see 1:2). Surrounded by vanity on all sides, the sage nevertheless offers the key to life. In a cosmos devoid of *telos* and a world filled with toil and frustration lies yet the triumph of living in the glory of the ordinary.

Ecclesiastes 12:9–14
Epilogue(s): The Edifying Ethos of Qoheleth

If there is any consensus among modern interpreters about Ecclesiastes, it is that the conclusion of the book does *not* comprise Qoheleth's own words. These final six verses are commonly considered the work of one or more epilogists, whose words both endorse and "conventionalize" the character and sayings of the sage. (Michael Fox is the notable exception, who contends that this unit is the product of the book's "narrator" ["Frame-Narrative and Composition in the Book of Qohelet," pp. 83–106].) In any case, the words of this postscript or addendum, cast in the third person (see also 1:1 and 7:27), are distinguished from Qoheleth's "own" words, which are frequently autobiographical in form. This "epilogue" serves both to confirm the sapiential character of the putative author and to bring his message into the biblical mainstream. The epilogist's words significantly qualify Qoheleth's own.

The first word of verse 9 signals the postscript status of the final verses: "Besides . . ." (cf. v. 12). Qoheleth, it is claimed, was both a scholar and a teacher, a natural combination in the business of wisdom. His vocation was to present wisdom in its various literary and aesthetic forms ("proverbs"), written and oral, in a thoroughly edifying way. Qoheleth exhibited a passion for pedagogy. The words of this ancient sage, thus, do not reflect some haphazard arrangement or whimsical purpose. They are arranged to instruct; his words are "pleasing" and "truthful," reflecting artistic and pedagogical care (v. 10). The "pleasing words" sought by the sage amid the cacophony of human discourse perhaps parallel Qoheleth's ardent search for joy amid the vanity of life. More broadly, a rhetorical elegance is claimed for the ancient sage's words, a craftsmanship that is inseparably wedded to the truth. Indeed, it is this intersection between aesthetics and truth, between elegance and aptness, that lies at the heart of the sapiential enterprise: "A word fitly spoken is like apples of gold in a setting of silver" (Prov. 25:11).

Yet that is not to say that the accumulated wisdom of the sages is easily digestible. The epilogist goes on to claim that there is nothing sugar-coated about *sapientia*. To the contrary, the sayings of the wise are likened to "goads" and "nails," painful prods (v. 11). Such images are drawn from the art of animal husbandry: "goads" were designed to herd domesticated animals, such as oxen (1 Sam. 13:21); "nails" were implanted at the end of sticks as prods. The "shepherd" or "herder" is evidently any teacher of wisdom, perhaps Qoheleth himself. Pain is part of the process of learning, analogous to the forceful training of animals. Had the epilogist wanted to convey a more *positive* sense of directive leadership, he or she could have easily employed the gentler images of rod and staff, also wielded by the shepherd (see Ps. 23:4). But as it stands, Ecclesiastes 12:11 acknowledges that the sage's words, consonant with much of sapiential instruction, sting! Perhaps Qoheleth's claim that "in much wisdom is much vexation, and those who increase knowledge increase sorrow" looms in the background (1:18). The path of wisdom is no road paved with gold. The trek can be tortuous, as Sirach, Qoheleth's noted successor, details: "At first [wisdom] will walk with them on tortuous paths . . . and will torment them by her discipline until she trusts them, and she will test them with her ordinances" (Sir. 4:17). The "goads" and "nails," in short, are the painful verbal instruments by which the purveyors of wisdom redirect the learner on the right path, rugged as it is.

To this ringing endorsement of Qoheleth's instruction, a caveat of sorts is appended (Eccl. 12:12–14). The (second?) epilogist warns that the reader must not go beyond Qoheleth's words. To do so only induces "weariness of the flesh." Far from denigrating his words, the statement carves out a preeminent place for Qoheleth's work, establishing his message as the final word on all matters pertaining to life and death. Ecclesiastes, in short, is the book to end all books. Yet, the epilogist laments, the production of written discourse continues unabated (1:4). The integrity of discourse is a favorite topic of Qoheleth (e.g., 5:1–3, 7 [Heb. 4:17—5:2, 6]; 10:12–14). The tendency to exploit discourse by multiplying it ad nauseum is Qoheleth's *bête noire*. Words can either build up or tear down, but quantity is no enhancement to their efficacy. To the contrary, the proliferation of words tends only to obfuscate clear thinking and right conduct. As conventional wisdom recognized long ago, discourse is a gift to be used only sparingly. The many schemes that plague human existence begin with increased verbiage; God made human beings straightforward and their discourse should reflect that (7:29; cf. 5:3 [Heb. v. 2]). And so it is with some degree of irony that the sage has chosen to express himself in frequently enigmatic and indirect

117

ways. Yet in all fairness, Qoheleth's legacy to posterity is remarkably terse. Compared to the monolithic work of Job or the baroque complexity of Proverbs, not to mention the voluminous works of their successors, Qoheleth's wisdom is powerfully conveyed in the smallest of sapiential packages.

In the spirit of simplicity, thus, one epilogist attempts to capture the thrust of Qoheleth's thought in the following double command: "Fear God and keep his commandments" (v. 13), remarkable in its terseness after "all has been heard." The latter phrase affirms what Qoheleth had insisted all along, namely, that he had seen and tested everything under the sun in the quest to arrive at an exhaustive inventory or "sum of things" (7:25; see also vv. 5, 23; 9:1; cf. 8:16–17). And, as a distillation of his observations, Qoheleth's short book says everything that requires saying, summed up now in a strikingly traditional imperative of reverence and obedience to God's commandments (cf. Deut. 5:29; 6:13, 24; 10:12–13, 20; 11:1; see also Sir. 1:26; 10:19; 23:27). For the epilogist, as for the Deuteronomist, true wisdom is displayed in obedience:

> You must observe [God's statutes and ordinances] diligently, for this will show your wisdom and discernment to the peoples, who, when they hear all these statutes, will say, "Surely this great nation is a wise and discerning people!" (Deut. 4:6)

The deuteronomic connection between wisdom and covenantal loyalty—referred almost interchangeably as "fear" and "love" in Deuteronomy (e.g., 6:4–5; 10:12–13; 11:1)—qualifies and restricts, but by no means contravenes, the theological core of Qoheleth's thought. The epilogist intends to demonstrate that as innovative as it is, the sage's message is hardly sui generis within the vast sweep of biblical tradition.

Godly fear, for example, is underscored four times by Qoheleth (3:14; 5:7 [Heb. v. 6]; 7:18; 8:12). For Qoheleth, reverence for God acknowledges the perdurability of divine power and activity, to which no agent, human or otherwise, can alter, much less resist (3:14; cf. Deut. 4:32–40). Reverential respect for God prompts a life of simplicity and moral integrity, as reflected in a person's discourse and conduct (Eccl. 5:7 [Heb. v. 6]). Qoheleth unwaveringly affirms that God holds people accountable for their actions. Divine reverence is the basis for maintaining ethical balance, avoiding the extremes of excessive wisdom and self-righteousness, on the one hand, and wickedness and folly, on the other (7:15–18). Indeed, there is a salutary efficacy associated with godly fear that resides, if not in reality, at least in the ancient sage's hope, and is closely aligned with his commendation of joy, a gift of God (8:10–15). In sum, "fear of God" connotes a reverence of the wholly Other that is devoid of grandiose expectations and cleansed of ulterior motives. It reflects a realistic faith at its simplest and sincerest level.

The epilogist's reference to following God's commandments as a necessary complement to divine reverence is missing in Qoheleth's presentation proper. Again, the language of 12:13 is more characteristic of deuteronomic discourse. Nevertheless, Qoheleth employs the language of obedience to highlight the binding import of the king's decree, a matter of discerning wisdom that is not unrelated to divine obedience: "the wise mind will know the time and way [for obeying a command]" (8:5). In addition, 12:13 serves to highlight certain core values that Qoheleth conveys in prescriptive form: simplicity in deed and integrity of word (5:1–7 [Heb. 4:17—5:6]), moderation in conduct and lack of presumption (7:15–20), and, of course, receiving and sharing joy (2:24–26; 3:12–13, 22; 5:18–20 [Heb. vv. 17–19]; 7:14; 8:15; 9:7–10; 11:1–2, 9–10). For all of Qoheleth's sapiential innovation, the epilogist aptly notes the centrality of divine reverence and obedience throughout the sage's reflections, while shrewdly moving the reader from Qoheleth's reflections to Torah obedience.

What is more, the epilogue calls to mind the natural connection between Qoheleth's instruction and divine judgment (12:14). In 11:9, which marks the sage's final commendation, Qoheleth invokes the severity of divine judgment in order to hold the youth accountable to the ways of joy and, thereby, to raise the bar of joy's standard to an ethical ideal. Elsewhere, Qoheleth asserts his confidence in God's discriminating judgment of the wicked and the righteous, a divinely appointed "time for every matter and for every work" (3:17; cf. 8:5–6). Divine judgment is what underwrites the inscrutable course of the cosmos (3:1, 11, 14–15). Time and season, life and death are governed by God's impenetrable determinations. Such judgments are not entirely retributive, Qoheleth observes; they are as inscrutable as they are unwavering. To God's unfathomable ways the epilogist appends a note about God's penetrating judgment on "every deed" (12:14). As piercing as the sun's heat, God's judgment penetrates both the deed and its underlying motives, bringing "every secret thing" to light (cf. 5:6 [Heb. v. 5], cf. Ps. 19:6, 12 [Heb. vv. 7, 13]). But for Qoheleth, the greatest secret is not the dark and turbid depths of the human heart, out of which innumerable schemes emerge (Eccl. 7:29), nor is it the indeterminate workings of the cosmos, which for all the toil seem to accomplish nothing (1:4–7). They all pale in comparison to the inscrutable Other, who remains in heaven yet holds humanity accountable and offers every good gift. God is the enigma above all others, the sovereignty of mystery. And yet, despite the insufferable vanity of life and death's dark victory, both the epilogist and the "Teacher" agree that God's justice, like the sure rising of "the sun of righteousness" (Mal. 4:2 [Heb. 3:20]), prevails (Eccl. 3:17; 8:12–13; 11:9). It is their hope against hope.

Epilogue
to the Commentary

Qoheleth's Place in Christian
Faith and Life

Taking my cue from Ecclesiastes 12:9–14, I find the genre of the epilogue to be the best place in which to express certain conclusions about Ecclesiastes from an expressly Christian perspective. As it behooved one early reader to clear the way for interpreting Qoheleth's discourse from a more orthodox perspective (v. 13), so I am compelled as a student of Scripture and one called into the body of Christ to discern constructive ways by which Christians can reflect upon and appropriate Ecclesiastes. It is no easy task. Interpreting Qoheleth's discourse from a Christian perspective cuts both ways. On the one hand, understanding Ecclesiastes theologically, rather than from a more disinterested standpoint, highlights particular aspects of the book while suppressing others. On the other hand, a serious grappling with Ecclesiastes underscores certain dimensions of the larger biblical witness that are too often overlooked. Such is the bane and blessing of interpreting Scripture as Scripture.

Finding a positive place in Christian theology for Qoheleth's wisdom—radical even by Old Testament standards—is, to put it mildly, a challenge. The temptation looms large among Christian interpreters to treat Qoheleth merely as a foil for the Gospel message, a deficient and dangerous perspective in dire need of rehabilitation. A recent example is found in the commentary by Tremper Longman. Longman considers Qoheleth as a "confused" and "despairing" sage who struggled mightily with traditional wisdom but without resolution (Longman, pp. 171, 188, 206, 261). All that redeems the book theologically, according to Longman, is the epilogue, which both affirms and critiques Qoheleth's words (12:9–14). Thus, he posits a sharp differentiation between the "theology of Qoheleth" and the "theology of the book," with the former serving essentially as a "foil" in the hands of the epilogist (Longman, pp. 38, 280). Compared with the redemptive message of the gospel, the world according to Qoheleth is set under curse and apart from God (Longman, pp. 39–40). Consequently, nothing positive can be said of Qoheleth's theology: "Life is full of trouble and then you die" (Longman, p. 34). Qoheleth's theological *coup de grâce* is his assertion that all life is "meaningless" (*hebel*).

While acknowledging that this is one way to read Ecclesiastes, I propose a more integrative approach toward incorporating Qoheleth's reflections into the fold of Christian discourse. By recognizing the book's canonical status, one must at some level concede that Ecclesiastes has something *integral* to say about faith seeking understanding. If anything, Qoheleth emphasizes the "seeking" dimension that is essential to faithful inquiry. As a seeker, Qoheleth sees himself on a journey toward understanding the totality of existence under God, of making sense of the world through the eyes of faith. Such an endeavor strikes at the heart and process of theological reflection.

The following observations, structured around pertinent themes, constitute a provisional attempt to discern how Qoheleth's thought is woven into some of the basic teachings of Scripture and, thus, into the heart and soul of Christian reflection. To be sure, Ecclesiastes by no means encapsulates the broad panorama of biblical faith from a canonical purview, but it does, I submit, make an indispensable contribution by adding a richness to the scriptural witness not otherwise found in any other book of the Bible. It would have been Scripture's loss had the early rabbis and church fathers decided against its inclusion into the canonical family (see Introduction). Ecclesiastes, even Qoheleth's theology, is thus no "treatise of straw," contrary to some modern interpreters (but not to Luther!).

Death

Perhaps the most troubling and obvious point of contention between Qoheleth and the Gospel message is the issue of the Resurrection. Simply put, for Qoheleth there is no life after death, let alone any discernment of some eschatological fulfillment to history. Qoheleth is a true believer in death and a cautious agnostic regarding the ultimate fate of the "human spirit" (Eccl. 3:21). Although the individual's life-breath ultimately returns to God (12:7), the preservation of the individual's identity, even what one might call a "soul," is mere wishful thinking in Qoheleth's eyes. In this sense, the sage is in line with most of Hebraic tradition. Yet for Qoheleth death denotes far more than physical extinction. It is the script of incertitude around which all of life is written. The foil of human existence, death denotes anything that contravenes human plans and activities. Indiscriminate by nature, death is the certitude of uncertainty, the impenetrable veil that at once conceals and seals human fate. Death, in short, crowns the hegemony of chance, and retribution has no place in its kingdom (see 9:11–12).

Despite appearances, Qoheleth's somber view of death and human destiny is not utterly alien to Christian reflection. The indiscriminate nature of fate is alluded to in Jesus' Sermon on the Mount: "[Your Father] makes his sun rise on the evil and on the good, and sends rain on the righteous and on the unrighteous" (Matt. 5:45). This sobering observation is, in fact, foundational to Jesus' command to "love your enemies." The love command, thus, has its home beyond the familiar expectations of divine retribution and blessing. That calamity smacks of senselessness is acknowledged by Jesus in Luke 13:1–5. Disaster does not seek out and strike the worst of sinners; all are susceptible (see Eccl. 9:11–12).

The future is unknown and beyond any mortal's control. Warning those who boast of their enterprising plans, James admonishes, "Yet you do not even know what tomorrow will bring. What is your life? For you are a mist that appears for a little while and then vanishes" (James 4:14). James' reference to "mist" (*atmis*) echoes, if not draws directly from, Qoheleth's frequent reference to *hebel*, literally "vapor," to denote in part the ephemeral nature of human existence. (See also the Codex Vaticanus translation of Eccl. 9:9 [*atmos*], as well as those of Aquila, Symmachus, and Theodotian of *hebel* throughout Ecclesiastes [*atmos, atmis*]). Certainty, or even confidence, about the future is rooted, according to James, in human arrogance (James 4:16). Like Qoheleth, James issues a blistering critique against those who are obsessed with acquiring wealth. Both the sage and the epistle writer associate seeking wealth with the woefully misguided attempt to wrest certainty out of uncertainty, like trying to drink water from a mirage or creating something out of nothing. Material plenty and lasting gain are secured by the one thing human beings will never grasp in their finitude: an inkling of the future. All that a stockbroker wants for Christmas is the next day's newspaper (only one will suffice!). But beating such odds boils down to outwitting death itself, the ultimate case of chasing after wind.

Death is real, Qoheleth avers, and he reminds the church that its veracity is in no way undercut by the Resurrection. Even in his proclamation on Christ's triumph over death, Paul does not gloss over the ravages of death: "for as all die in Adam, so all will be made alive in Christ" (1 Cor. 15:22). Life, even new life, cannot exist without death. Being made alive in Christ is essentially a "postmortem" event, as Paul admonishes those who speculate about the resurrected body: "Fool! What you sow does not come to life unless it dies" (v. 36). Or as Jesus, according to John, succinctly states, "Very truly, I tell you, unless a grain

123

of wheat falls into the earth and dies, it remains just a single grain; but if it dies, it bears much fruit" (John 12:24). The reality of death, though recast, remains alive and well. To be sure, death is no longer the final word in light of the Resurrection, but it does remain indomitable to human control, which is the upshot of Qoheleth's morbid reflections (e.g., Eccl. 8:8). There are those, Paul observed, who "say there is no resurrection" (1 Cor. 15:12). Conversely, there are plenty inside and outside the church today who claim there is no death in Christ. Despite all docetic reformulations to the contrary, ancient and modern, Jesus died. And the full acknowledgement of his death is essential to the rite of baptism, in which recipients become buried with Christ in death as much as they are raised with Christ to "newness of life" (Rom. 6:3–4). Death is still the necessary threshold for the human spirit to "return to God who gave it" (Eccl. 12:7).

Acceptance of death marks the supreme surrender of control for Qoheleth. Death is the altar upon which all ambition and pride are sacrificed. Particularly in a death-defying culture such as ours, the surrender to death, and thus to God, is nothing less than a theological imperative. It is the way of the cross. In a provocative manner that Qoheleth himself might have approved, Jesus in John's Gospel reflects ethically on the necessity of death: "Those who love their life lose it, and those who hate their life in this world will keep it. . . ." (John 12:25; cf. Matt. 10:39; Mark 8:35; Luke 17:33). For the sage who "hated life" (Eccl. 2:17), surrendering wealth and ambition, indeed his very substance, marked the first step toward his affirmation of life, of life lived in receiving the gifts of joy. Such was Qoheleth's redemption, it could be said. For Paul and the Gospel writers, the joy of the Resurrection brings such redemption to its consummation.

The Purpose of History

As "the mother of Christian theology," apocalyptic characterizes much of early Christian thought, particularly Paul's, as Ernst Käsemann points out. Yet such a theology seems utterly alien to Qoheleth's worldview. Distinctly lacking in Qoheleth's anthropology is any sense of purpose to history, apocalyptic or prophetic. Death exposes all hope for a progressive purpose in human history as chimerical. Any hint of a *telos* in history, cosmic or human, is simply a mirage, "vanity" (see 3:1–11). Nevertheless, Paul borrows directly from Qoheleth's language to set the scene for the consummation of God's glory in Rom. 8:19–20:

For the creation waits with eager longing for the revealing of the children of God; for the creation was subjected to futility [*mataiotēti*], not of its own will but by the will of the one who subjected it, in hope [*eph' helpidi*] that the creation itself will be set free from its bondage to decay and will obtain the freedom of the glory of the children of God.

It is no coincidence that Paul's term for "futility" (*mataiotēs*) is identical to the Old Greek's translation of *hebel* in Qoheleth (see Longman, pp. 39–40). Indeed, for both Paul and Qoheleth, "vanity" does not mark a world *without* God; it marks a world *subjected by* God. Along with Paul, Qoheleth attributes the absurdity of existence to God's sovereignty over creation. But for Paul, the *via dolorosa* of cosmic and human history has become purposeful: "vanity" engenders solidarity with a world in bondage to decay and in hope for its freedom (vv. 22–25). Here, too, Qoheleth subtly confirms Paul's vision: the individual and the cosmic share an inseparable destiny. Moreover, there is "hope" for the living (Eccl. 9:4). Far from optimism, Qoheleth's "hope" is informed by the certitude of death and is bound up with the passionate desire for life among the living.

As Vaclav Havel notes, "[Hope] is not the conviction that something will turn out well, but the certainty that something makes sense, regardless of how it turns out. . . . [I]t is something we get, as it were, from 'elsewhere'" (Havel, pp. 181–82). For the apostle, such hope is born from suffering and vindicated by the world's consummation (Rom. 5:3–4). The world according to Qoheleth is Paul's point of departure for describing the glorious freedom that all the world will enjoy in due time, a time entirely appropriate, but one that no mortal can predict (see Eccl. 3:11; Luke 12:40). Qoheleth has unwittingly set the stage for such an apocalyptic encounter. It is the cross that history has borne from time immemorial. It is the cross that God has borne in Christ's death. It is the cross that paves the way for freedom from "bondage to decay."

Gain and Gift, Joy and Sorrow

As death is the crowning testimony that humanity cannot save itself, the human incapacity to achieve lasting gain is its corollary, the center of Qoheleth's message. "What do people gain from all the toil at which they toil under the sun?" (Eccl. 1:3). The sage's answer is loud and clear: "nothing" (2:11). Jesus poses a similar question about those who seek to save their lives: "[W]hat will it profit them if they gain the whole world but forfeit their life?" (Matt. 16:26). Qoheleth's answer has not changed. Earthly treasures are consumed, not by their owners but by "moth and rust" (Matt. 6:19). Striving after wealth, both the sage and the evangelist aver, only displaces divine reverence (Eccl. 5:10–20 [Heb. vv. 9–19]; Matt. 6:24). If anything, the Gospel writers radicalize

125

Qoheleth's thought in their condemnation of striving after material possessions, even for the basic means of human sustenance, and by exposing the drive toward consumption as a symptom of anxiety (Matt. 6:25–34; Luke 12:22–30). Yet there remains one true thing for which to strive, the Gospel writers agree: the kingdom of God, which requires a striving that is unlike any other and receives a gain unlike any other (Matt. 6:33; Luke 12:31).

In Matthew's parable of the vineyard laborers, those "who have borne the burden of the day and the scorching heat" look on with envy (literally with an "evil eye") at those who receive the same wage yet have worked no more than an hour (Matt. 20:1–16). With similar disgust, Qoheleth bitterly laments the prospect of a stranger receiving the fruits of his toiling "under the sun" (Eccl. 2:18–21; 6:1–2). The parable underscores an indiscriminate mercy that overcomes the strictures of conventional fairness. While Qoheleth would count it as a travesty, Matthew chalks it up as the scandal of the good news. From either perspective, however, a lesson rings loud and clear: "[O]ne's life does not consist in the abundance of possessions" (Luke 12:15). Luke's parable of the rich fool draws from Qoheleth's negative view of wealth. Facing death, the man who built bigger barns to store his surplus is admonished by God, not because he planned to "relax, eat, drink, [and] be merry"—Luke's ironic use of Qoheleth's commendation of joy (see also Isa. 22:13; Tobit 7:10; 1 Cor. 15:32)—but because he greedily strove for more material abundance. "And the things you have prepared, whose will they be?" God asks. Qoheleth knows. Once again, death divests life of all its material accounts. "For the sun rises with its scorching heat and withers the field. . . . It is the same way with the rich; in the midst of a busy life, they will wither away" (James 1:11). Such is the "busy-ness" of striving.

Both Qoheleth and the Gospel writers agree: life is more than gain; it is a gift. Thus, one's true vocation is more than material striving; it is sharing and receiving (see Eccl. 11:1–2). "Do not be afraid, little flock, for it is your Father's good pleasure to give you the kingdom" (Luke 12:32). God's favor is unearned and unpossessed; it, too, is a gift (see also 2 Cor. 9:8). For Paul, the gift of grace in Christ is nothing short of "indescribable," prompting a lifelong exercise in thanksgiving to God (v. 14). More gift than gain, Christ subverts and transforms the natural pursuit of gain. As Paul confesses:

126

[W]hatever *gains* I had, these I have come to regard as *loss* because of Christ. More than that, I regard everything as *loss* because of the surpassing value of knowing Christ Jesus my Lord. For his sake I have suffered the *loss* of all things, and I regard them as rubbish, in order that I may *gain* Christ." (Phil. 3:7–8; italics added)

Christ is the world's true gain, a gain like no other, imperishable and undeserved, gifted and grace-filled, exposing all other gains as worthless objects of futile striving.

The gift of enjoyment and the futility of gain are two sides of the same coin of Qoheleth's message. For the ancient sage, the simplicity of joy is more than a "narcotic" (so Longman, p. 35) or an "antidote" (so Seow, *Ecclesiastes*, p. 157). It provides more than just psychological relief. The fact that Qoheleth's taxonomy of joy includes not only the delights of basic sustenance ("eating" and "drinking") but also work and community (e.g., Eccl. 3:22; 9:7–10) suggests otherwise. Moreover, the sage discerns an intimate connection between sorrow and joy (7:3). Receiving joy and striving for gain represent two diametrically opposed life orientations: one rushes headlong into the ever elusive future, and the other anchors itself in the inescapable present. Far from being an escape, joy is nothing less than Qoheleth's solution to the crisis of life, its "vanity." The enemies of life, anxiety and worry, have no place in a life that orients itself around the joys of the present. Such advice is echoed in the Sermon on the Mount: "So do not worry about tomorrow, for tomorrow will bring worries of its own. Today's trouble is enough for today" (Matt. 6:34). Luke puts it even more sharply when Jesus asks rhetorically, "And can any of you by worrying add a single hour to your span of life?" (Luke 12:25).

The fact that the New Testament abounds with admonitions to rejoice makes Ecclesiastes a strange bedfellow in the canonical family, as strange perhaps as its liturgical association with the Jewish Feast of Booths (see Introduction). Nevertheless, both Qoheleth and the apostolic witness recognize that joy can be given, even demanded, but never possessed. As Paul Tillich succinctly states, "[Joy] is not easy to attain. It is and always was a rare and precious thing. And it has always been a difficult problem among Christians. Christians are accused of destroying the joy of life, this natural endowment of every creature" (Tillich, p. 142). Perhaps it takes, of all people, a dour sage to teach Christians a thing or two about joy!

Qoheleth reminds the church that joy is not an otherworldly reality, something deferred until after death. Joy in Christ embraces joy within one's life, created and sustained by God. Joy is not a matter of gaining control over someone or something else for the purpose of deriving pleasure. To the contrary, joy is a gift, one that can even coexist with sorrow, its opposite, as the ancient sage suggests (Eccl. 7:3). In the

127

movie *Shadowlands,* which recounts the relationship between C. S. Lewis and his wife, Joy, Lewis expresses his fear of the sorrow he will feel when he loses Joy, who is stricken with terminal bone cancer. Joy responds: "The pain then is a part of the pleasure now. That's the deal" (Meilaender, p. 31). Qoheleth tells us that such a "deal" is set for us all. The joy of the moment is heightened all the more by the realization that it will not last. Jesus, too, reminds his disciples of the sorrow that is to come when he must depart. But that is not all: he tells his disciples that their pain "will turn into joy" (John 16:20). "Ask and you will receive, so that your joy may be complete," Jesus enjoins (v. 24). Joy is imparted and received, not attained and possessed.

For Qoheleth, it is no coincidence that the most tangible setting for joy is found around a table. The sage presupposes a context of fellowship when he commends the delight of "eating and drinking." By contrast, those who "eat in darkness, in much vexation and sickness and resentment" are condemned by their own efforts to eat in isolation and despair for having striven for wealth (Eccl. 5:15, 17 [Heb. vv. 14, 16]). Qoheleth, thus, places great value upon ordinary table fellowship.

Not fortuitously, table fellowship is a central theme and context for Jesus' ministry. "The Son of Man came eating and drinking, and they say, 'Look, a glutton and a drunkard, a friend of tax collectors and sinners!'" Jesus quotes his detractors, "Yet wisdom is vindicated by her deeds" (Matt. 11:19). Next to inclusiveness, the most prominent characteristic of table fellowship in the New Testament is joy (Bolyki, p. 228). Luke, moreover, equates Jesus' table fellowship with the eschatological kingdom of God (Luke 13:29; 22:30). In Luke's parable of the great banquet, the most prominent excuse given by those who decline the invitation to the feast is their attention to their possessions (14:18–19)! Companionship with Jesus, in short, is a matter not simply of the heart; it is a communion in the most palpable sense: "Behold, I stand at the door and knock; if you hear my voice and open the door, I will come in to you and eat with you, and you with me" (Rev. 3:20 [an adaptation of the RSV and NRSV]).

For Qoheleth, those who continually strive for possessions bar the door, in effect, and thereby forsake the joy that is found within the most ordinary and natural of events in the daily rhythm of life. Ordinary joy reveals the giftedness of life. "The very commonness of everyday things harbors the eternal marvel and silent mystery of God," notes Karl Rahner (Rahner, p. 14). Through his disillusionment, Qoheleth comes to discern the glory of the ordinary, made tangibly palpable in the regular gathering for a common meal. It is no accident, then, that for the New Testament the very consummation of history is centered around a table, as prefigured in the Lord's Supper (Matt. 11:19; 22:1–14; 26:29; Rev. 19:9). Every time communion is celebrated, Christians remember Christ's death and resurrection as well as look forward to that day when they will sit down to supper at table with their Lord in the Kingdom.

Table fellowship, moreover, has its own peculiar ethos. Paul exhorts the Corinthian congregation, "Do not seek your own advantage, but that of the other" (1 Cor. 10:24). At the Lord's Table, all self-striving is banished. Acknowledging the fellowship and unity of the body—the church—is paramount, "for all who eat and drink without discerning the body, eat and drink judgment against themselves," Paul warns (11:29). The integrity of the Table rests in part on the quality of fellowship and hospitality (cf. James 2:1–7), values that Qoheleth himself espouses: bread is to be eaten in joy as well as given in hospitality (Eccl. 9:7; 11:1–2). As the Eucharist is the supreme act of fellowship and joy in community, so "eating and drinking" for Qoheleth is the communal embodiment of the joy that comes "from the hand of God" (Eccl. 2:24b). While the Lord's Supper points both backward and forward within the larger scheme of divine providence, Qoheleth reminds Christians that its most immediate context is the here-and-now with Christ, the present in the abiding presence of the Other. "Rejoice in the Lord always" is Paul's concluding exhortation to the Philippians, for "the Lord is near" (Phil. 4:4–5). It is precisely God's nearness that Paul regards as the greatest gift. And it is precisely in the joy of the immanent that Qoheleth most fully discerns God's gifted presence (see below).

Work and Vocation

Qoheleth's taxonomy of joy includes, rather than rejects, the value of work. The issue of work commends itself as an issue of ethical reflection for Christians today as it did for the ancients. Work, or in Qoheleth's language "toil," is a quintessentially human activity. As Heidi Hadsell points out, work "is also the principal activity through which humanity participates in creation" (Hadsell, p. 98). It is no wonder, then, that Qoheleth discerns a natural link between the workings of the cosmos and the daily toil (and trials) of human beings (see 1:3–8). The state of the cosmos reflects the state of human affairs and vice versa.

Qoheleth's testimony forces a revaluation of work. The effort human beings expend to achieve lasting gain or advantage, the sage coolly observes, is all for naught. Lasting gain, profit, or self-advantage remains ever beyond one's reach. Yet Qoheleth does not disparage work. To the contrary, it is for him an ethical duty: "Whatever your hand finds to do, do with your might; for there is no work or thought or knowledge or wisdom in Sheol, to which you are going" (9:10). Without the

129

prospect of profit, the value of work is recast but not rejected. As a means to self-advantage, whether monetary or "moral," work paradoxically becomes self-demoralizing: "For whom am I toiling . . . and depriving myself of pleasure?" laments the loner (4:8). "Do not be too righteous, and do not act too wise; why should you destroy yourself?" Qoheleth rhetorically asks (7:16).

In today's market-driven economy, the exclusive focus on profit invariably reduces work to a mere job—Qoheleth's oppressive "toil"—and a job is no vocation. With such a focus, the job itself becomes meaningless, except for the compensation one receives. More pernicious is the economic value placed on a person's job, which invariably determines the social and ethical value of that person. Hadsell's assessment that work today, as typically construed in American society, encourages only alienating individualism is nothing new (Hadsell, p. 102); it is something Qoheleth himself laments. For the sage, work is redeemed both by community and by its very nature as an exercise of human dignity before death makes its irrevocable claim. Qoheleth places the value of work on the same par with the eminently social delights of eating and drinking (see 9:7–10). Meaningful work is not driven by envy of another or by self-advantage, not even by achievement (4:4, 7–8). It is a gift and a vocation. Like Qoheleth, Calvin considered work as the primary activity of human participation in the social world and is rightfully famous for the positive value he placed on it, much in contrast to the cultural norms of his day (Hadsell, pp. 98–99). Both the ancient sage and the French reformer regarded work as a right and ethical duty, never an option.

Qoheleth's view of work is liberating for today's men and women. Christian counselor James Dittes points out that true "liberation from work" does not mean settling for early retirement. What it does involve is correcting the fundamental misconception that work is done simply "in order to achieve something." He goes on to say: "It is the intensity of directing, of aiming at a target, the intensity of needing to produce or accomplish something—that is what sets up work to go sour" (Dittes, pp. 87–88). Dittes likens all-consuming work to a love affair gone awry. Such is precisely Qoheleth's point. Like Qoheleth, Dittes finds the value of teamwork over and against competition as essential in liberating the kind of work ethic that tends to enslave rather than enliven (Dittes, pp. 90–91). The secret for Qoheleth lies in recognizing that one works not for self-gain but for the thrill of applying one's gifts and talents for the sake of another without any self-driven expectations of the results.

130   Qoheleth's outward-turning perspective on work informs much of Christian vocation in particular. Paul echoes the sentiments of Qoheleth: "So whether you eat or drink, or whatever you do, do everything

for the glory of God. . . . I try to please everyone in everything I do, not seeking my own advantage, but that of many, so that they may be saved" (1 Cor. 10:31–33). Paul opens his exhortation on Christian vocation in a way that distinctly recalls the language of Eccl. 9:10a. Like the sage, Paul, too, places work on par with table fellowship and preserves his sense of vocation from any taint of self-advantage. The "glory of God" sets a new direction for work, turning it outward toward the "advantage of the many." Set in its proper communal context, work is an offering to God in thanksgiving that involves the right stewardship of one's gifts and talents for the benefit of the other. There is, thus, a striving that is appropriate to the work of the kingdom, but it is far from self-striving: "[S]trive first for the kingdom of God . . . and all these things will be given to you as well" (Matt. 6:33; see Luke 12:30).

For Qoheleth, "striving" is intractably self-referential and ultimately self-demoralizing. Paul and the Gospel writers, however, allow for a certain kind of striving, but one that is radically redefined as an exercise in self-giving. Both the ancient sage and the New Testament authors recognize that meaningful work must be divested from the lures of self-advancement; it is a gift of God to be given. "[I]f they fall, one will lift up the other," Qoheleth observes about the value of collaboration (Eccl. 4:10a). For the sage, labor is rewarding only insofar that it is done in community. In the context of fellowship and self-giving, toil finds its true place, far removed from any hint of works righteousness (see 7:16). Addressing the Corinthians about the resurrection, Paul declares, "[I]n the Lord your labor is not in vain" (1 Cor. 15:58). For Qoheleth, the vanity of toil rests on the elusiveness of self-gain. Paul does not deny this; indeed, he presupposes it! For the apostle, labor that is "not in vain" is labor done "in service" rather than for self-advantage (16:16). As Qoheleth vividly points out, work for self-gain is the harshest taskmaster (Eccl. 4:7–8). But service for another in the spirit of Christian discipleship is an entirely different matter:

> Come to me, all you that are weary and are carrying heavy burdens, and I will give you rest. Take my yoke upon you, and learn from me; for I am gentle and humble in heart, and you will find rest for your souls. For my yoke is easy, and my burden is light. (Matt. 11:28–30)

Like Jesus' invitation, Qoheleth's commendation of rest and joy is a lesson in wisdom (see Sir. 51:26–27).

Qoheleth's indictment of self-achievement is consonant with much of Scripture—from the garden and Tower of Babel stories in Genesis to the apocalypse of Revelation. All insist upon the limitations of human power and the temptations of self-deception. Human identity does

131

not rest on achievements. A person is more than the sum of his or her successes and failures. The message of Scripture is that one need not be enslaved or alienated by the toil of work, for human identity and destiny rest on what God does and has done, rather than on what human beings strive to achieve. Created in the image of God, humankind *shares* in God's own creative activity, both in work and in rest. Rather than absorbed in their own achievements, human beings find their true vocation in discipleship.

> The kingdom of heaven is like treasure hidden in a field, which someone found and hid; then in his *joy* he goes and sells all that he has and buys that field. Again, the kingdom of heaven is like a merchant in search of fine pearls; on finding one pearl of great value, he went and sold all that he had and bought it. (Matt. 13:44–46; italics added)

The kingdom of God comes not as a demand but as a gift. Work "in the Lord," rather than in one's self, is work's joyous gift, discipleship. As gift and work fit hand-in-glove for the ancient sage, so the apostle regards Israel's very calling or vocation as an irrevocable gift of God's grace (Rom. 11:29). Paul and Qoheleth remind us that the kingdom of God is not built brick by brick. God's commonwealth is already established, ready to be received as the one true object of our striving. If the kingdom of God is indeed mirrored in table fellowship (see above), then the kingdom's work is best captured in the setting of the table to which all are invited by Jesus, the Host.

Knowledge of God

Qoheleth's depiction of God seems quite at odds with New Testament portrayals. Longman, for example, notes that for the ancient sage "God [is] distant, occasionally indifferent, and sometimes cruel," in a word, a terrifying deity (Longman, pp. 35–36). Such a statement might be an accurate appraisal in light of a few isolated references the sage makes about God. But Qoheleth presents us with a fuller and more nuanced portrayal. To be sure, God acts as judge (Eccl. 3:14), imparts wrath as well as favor (2:24), and inspires "fear" (3:11; 5:7 [Heb. v. 6]; 8:12)—themes that find corresponding references in New Testament literature (e.g., Rom. 1:18; 2:16; 9:22; 2 Cor. 7:1; 2 Tim. 4:8; Heb. 10:30; 12:23; Rev. 6:16–17; 14:7). But to be fair to Qoheleth, any interpreter must also come to terms with the more positive sides of God's character and activity indicated in Ecclesiastes. God is the author of the "day of prosperity" (Eccl. 7:14). Every good gift comes from the "hand of God," including the very capacity for enjoyment (2:24; 3:12–13; 5:19 [Heb. v. 18]) and the capacity to work (3:22; 9:10). God, moreover, is the creator of life (12:1).

By claiming that God creates both the "day of prosperity" and the "day of adversity," Qoheleth underscores the mystery of divine sovereignty. And yet the sage discerns the hint of a rationale behind the sovereignty, one that bears significant pedagogical implications: "God has made the one as well as the other, so that mortals may not find out anything that will come after them" (7:14b; see 10:14b). Inscrutable in character, divine sovereignty shrouds all knowledge, casting a thick blanket of incognizance over human perception. The sage's theological anthropology turns on a low and limiting view of human nature: "God made human beings straightforward, but they have devised many schemes" (7:29). But God trumps all human activity and goals, exposing them as illusions of presumption. God, thus, is wholly Other and human beings must acknowledge their finitude in all thought and conduct: "God is in heaven, and you upon earth; therefore let your words be few" (5:2 [Heb. v. 1]). For Qoheleth, the moral payoff of divine transcendence is restraint in speech. Such discursive reserve is also commanded, not fortuitously, by Jesus in the Sermon on the Mount for somewhat similar reasons: "Do not swear at all, either by heaven, for it is the throne of God, or by the earth, for it is his footstool. . . . Let your word be 'Yes, Yes' or 'No, No'; anything more than this comes from the evil one" (Matt. 5:34–35, 37; see also James 5:12). Qoheleth would lodge the "evil one" within humankind's own conflictive nature. Humankind is its own worst enemy. Far from advocating nihilism, the sage exhorts his readers to take responsibility for themselves. Approach the terrible throne of grace not with a proliferation of excuses and ulterior motives, but with "calmness" and acceptance, Qoheleth would enjoin (see Eccl. 9:4).

Shrouded in mystery, God is free from human manipulation, not at the expense but in full acknowledgement of humanity's frail identity. Qoheleth's ethics is based on a self-critical theological modesty; an orientation that is honest to an inscrutable God and world. For Qoheleth, the earth is not full of the "knowledge of the Lord as the waters cover the sea," as claimed in Isa. 11:9. Rather, the world is veiled with vanity as a shroud covers a corpse. "You do not know the work of God, who makes everything," Qoheleth admonishes those who would presume differently (11:5). Indeed, to think otherwise is worse than speculation; it is the height of hubris. To presume to penetrate the mind of God exceeds the bounds of human finitude.

The sage preserves on behalf of divine reverence an acute awareness of mystery, which serves to safeguard all knowledge from the scourge of presumption. Such awareness should never be denied in Christian reflection on the nature of revelation. That Qoheleth found wisdom to be "far off, and deep, very deep" sets the stage for the disclosure, in Paul's words, of the "mystery that was kept secret for long ages" (Rom. 16:25). Mystery is still preserved, even in revelation's disclosure. The wisdom of God is "secret and hidden" (1 Cor. 2:10). By vanity, Qoheleth would say, God has "made foolish the wisdom of the world." That "vanity," Paul would say, is Christ, who exposes the "wisdom of the wise" (1:18–25). As Qoheleth, for all his acquired wisdom, saw himself no different than a fool, Paul regards his message as the proclamation of "foolishness," worn as a badge of honor (v. 21). The gospel is the "mystery of Christ" (Eph. 3:4). As a "steward of God's mysteries," one must handle "God's foolishness" with care. With Qoheleth's skepticism lurking in the background, Paul must admit: "For now we see in a mirror, dimly, but then we will see face to face. Now I know only in part; then I will know fully, even as I have been fully known" (1 Cor. 13:12). Indeed, by God's providence, knowledge "will come to an end" (v. 8), as in fact it already has for Qoheleth. In the end, the practice ("love"), rather than the wisdom, abides.

Yes, Qoheleth's God seems distant and inscrutable, even absent, and yet the sage readily discerns the "hand of God" as he savors the all-too-fleeting moments of joy (Eccl. 2:24). Qoheleth's God is not the God of mighty deeds who would vanquish enemies or release the oppressed with a strong and mighty arm. No, the God of this sage lets well enough alone. The sage had attempted to discern God in the grand design of the universe and history, no less, but failed. Not the *mighty* acts but the *minor* acts of God is the theological focus of Qoheleth's testimony. Transcendent and immanent, absent yet subtly present is Qoheleth's God (so also Gorssen, pp. 314–15). His God is found not in the grand scheme of things but in the details of a life fully lived, fully enjoyed, fully surrendered, a life lost to vanity, a life received in gratitude. God's hand remains open, not to break into history to crush a foe or break one's bonds, but to offer the simple gifts of sustenance and joy. This God is the God of small things. This God is also the God in Christ. Dietrich Bonhoeffer provocatively captures this paradox of God's absence and immanence in everyday living:

> [W]e cannot be honest unless we recognize that we have to live in the world *etsi deus non daretur*. . . . So our coming of age leads us to a true recognition of our situation before God. God would have us know what we must live as [those] who manage our lives without him. The God who is with us is the God who forsakes us (Mark 15.34). The God who lets us live in the world without the working hypothesis of God is the God before whom we stand still continually. Before God and with God we live without God. God lets himself be pushed out of the world on to the cross. (Bonhoeffer, p. 360)

For the ancient sage, God's absence is wholly rooted in God's otherness (Eccl. 5:2 [Heb. v. 1]). Such stress may remind readers of the modern theologian Karl Barth. Considered too gloomy by many of his contemporaries, Barth was considered by Bonhoeffer to embody true *hilaritas* (Bethge, p. 52). John Updike, too, was surprised that a theologian, of all people, could so wholeheartedly enjoy living in the world:

> Karl Barth's insistence on the otherness of God seemed to free him to be exceptionally (for a theologian) appreciative and indulgent of this world, the world at hand. His humor and love of combat, his capacity for friendship even with his ideological opponents, his fondness for tobacco and other physical comforts, his tastes in art and entertainment were heartily worldly, worldly not in the fashion of those who accept this life as a way-station and testing ground but of those who embrace it as a piece of Creation. (Updike, p. 7)

The same could be said of Qoheleth, this teacher of joy amid the woe. Far from cultivating a life of austerity and gloom, the sage's ruminations commend a life of enjoyment under (and by virtue of) the inscrutably sovereign Other: "Go, eat your bread with enjoyment, and drink your wine with a merry heart; for God has long ago approved what you do" (Eccl. 9:7).

Knowledge of Self

With knowledge of God there is also knowledge of the self, and for Qoheleth the lack of certainty cuts both ways. For the first two chapters, the "Teacher" effectively deconstructs his royal, Solomonic identity, and casts himself among the common lot of humanity, finite and frail that it is. Qoheleth is both sage and commoner, student and teacher, skeptic and servant, victor and failure. He rages and expresses resignation; he laughs and despairs; he is dispassionate at one point and anguished at another (e.g., 4:1); he boasts as well as deprecates himself. The sage assumes all these identities and covers the gamut of human experience so that his readers may be instructed. Paul, too, became "all things to all people, that [he] might by all means save some" (1 Cor. 9:22).

The sage's ever-shifting character, however, is not simply a pedagogical tool; it reflects a crisis of identity. Who is Qoheleth, this man of joy and woe? What is humanity, afflicted with both frailty and the capacity for self-transcendence? The sage cannot confidently echo the answer given in Psalm 8, which boasts that human beings have been made "a little lower than God, and crowned them with glory and honor" (Ps. 8:5). Crowned with thorns, more likely, Qoheleth would suggest. Yet in the background, the sage does seem to ponder the psalmist's question

135

"What are human beings that you are mindful of them, mortals that you care for them?" (v. 4). Finite and frail, full of schemes and inclined toward evil (Eccl. 7:29; 8:11), who are these creatures to whom the sovereign, inscrutable God bestows the gifts of joy and sustenance amid life's heavy burdens? This, too, is a mystery. The sage, like Bonhoeffer, realized that something more is at stake than self-knowledge:

> Who am I? This or the other?
> Am I one person today, and tomorrow another?
> Am I both at once? A hypocrite before others,
> and before myself a contemptible woebegon weakling?
> Or is something within me still like a beaten army,
> fleeing in disorder from victory already achieved?
>
> Who am I? They mock me, these lonely questions of mine.
> Whoever I am, thou knowest, O God, I am thine.
>
> (Bonhoeffer, p. 348)

Qoheleth, too, knows to whom he belongs.

Conclusion

H. W. Hertzberg, at the conclusion of his commentary, speaks for many an exegete when he notes that in Qoheleth's profile of *hebel* the "Old Testament was here at the point of running itself to death. Yet behind this total nothingness [i.e., *hebel*] from the human perspective was as its only possible help the 'new creature' of the New Testament" (Hertzberg, p. 237). My reflections given above are cast in the hope that there is indeed something *within* this "total nothingness," not behind it or above it, that adumbrates the new creation. A Christian reading of Ecclesiastes, in other words, need not dismiss Qoheleth's message as simply a foil for the gospel. It is very possible that James and Paul, if not the Gospel writers and Jesus himself, were steeped in the language and ethos of this canonical misfit. That is not to say that Ecclesiastes, or any other book of the Bible for that matter, contains all in all. Indeed, more than Qoheleth's imagination could ever muster, the eyes of faith can stare resolutely at the stranger whom the sage viewed with contempt and see in this figure intimations of Christ, to whom everything is given. That Christ, too, suffered the ravages of "vanity" reveals the Stranger not as the world's threat but as its greatest gift.

A student recently told me about a friend of hers who had just finished reading Ecclesiastes and remarked that the book "makes everything OK." There may be more truth to that response than all the commentaries and scholarly studies put together. To this "untrained eye," how can a book so laden with the oppressive weight of weariness and so filled with the stench of death offer a word of consolation or even something redemptive? One can only imagine. Perhaps because Qoheleth begins with mundane experience and crafts a way of life that acknowledges in full both the dread and the delight of it all. Perhaps because Qoheleth can make the move from misery to mystery without falling into the pit of despair. Maybe because Qoheleth, for all his self-acclaimed acuity and accomplishments, turns out to be a humble searcher for truth and dignity, a casualty of his ambitions yet a recipient of life's ordinary gifts. Or perhaps because the words of this consummate sage resonate with us all, believer and skeptic, optimist and pessimist, realist and idealist, with his unflinching view of life in all its absurdity and obscurity and show us a way to come to terms, which is no easy feat.

With anguished tears, Qoheleth has baptized the irrational world of experience. For those who hold out against the empirical odds for something greater, for some redemptive good that lies beyond the vain world as we know it, the sage reminds us that there is plenty already under our noses. Ecclesiastes recounts the journey of an ancient sage who returns not only empty-handed in his ambitious quest to figure out life but also open-handed to the God of the simple gifts. "Today's trouble is enough for today," Jesus concludes (Matt. 6:34). And so also is today's gift, the sage confirms.

BIBLIOGRAPHY

For further study

Barton, George A. *A Critical and Exegetical Commentary on the Book of Ecclesiastes.* International Critical Commentary. Edinburgh: T. & T. Clark, 1908.

Barucq, André. *Ecclésiate.* Verbum Satutis 3. Paris: Beauchesne, 1968.

Crenshaw, James L. *Old Testament Wisdom: An Introduction.* 2d ed. Louisville: Westminster John Knox, 1998.

————. "Youth and Old Age in Qoheleth," *Hebrew Annual Review* 11(1987):1–13.

————. "Qoheleth in Current Research," *Hebrew Annual Review* 7(1983):41–56.

————. "The Shadow of Death in Qoheleth." In *Israelite Wisdom: Theological and Literary Essays in Honor of Samuel Terrien,* edited by J. G. Gammie, 205–16. Missoula, Mont.: Scholars Press, 1978.

Fox, Michael V. *A Time to Tear Down and a Time to Build Up: A Rereading of Ecclesiastes.* Grand Rapids: Wm. B. Eerdmans, 1999.

————. "Wisdom in Qoheleth." In *In Search of Wisdom: Essays in Memory of John G. Gammie,* edited by Leo G. Perdue *et al.,* 115–31. Louisville: Westminster/John Knox, 1993.

————. *Qohelet and His Contradictions.* Bible and Literature Series 18. Sheffield: Almond, 1989.

Gese, Hartmut. "The Crisis of Wisdom in Koheleth." In *Theodicy in the Old Testament,* edited by James L. Crenshaw, Issues in Religion and Theology 4, 141–53, 1963. Philadelphia: Fortress, 1983.

Lauha, Aarre. *Kohelet.* Biblischer Kommentar: Altes Testament 19. Neukirchen-Vluyn: Neukirchener, 1978.

Loader, J. A. *Ecclesiastes: A Practical Commentary.* Text and Interpretation. Grand Rapids: Wm. B. Eerdmans, 1986.

Lohfink, Norbert. *Kohelet.* Die Neue Echter Bible. Würzberg: Echter, 1980.

Luther, Martin. "Notes on Ecclesiastes." In *Luther's Works,* vol. 15, edited and translated by J. Pelikan, 3–193. Saint Louis: Concordia, 1972.

Michel, Diethelm. "Vom Gott, der im Himmel ist (Reden von Gott bei Qohelet)," *Theologia Viatorum* 12(1973/74):87–100.

Murphy, Roland E. *The Tree of Life: An Exploration of Biblical Wisdom Literature.* 2d ed. Grand Rapids: Wm. B. Eerdmans, 1996.

———. "Qoheleth and Theology?" *Biblical Theology Bulletin* 21(1991):30–33.

———. "The Sage in Ecclesiastes and Qoheleth the Sage." In *The Sage in Israel and the Ancient Near East,* edited by John G. Gammie and Leo G. Perdue, 263–71. Winona Lake, Ind.: Eisenbrauns, 1990.

———. "The Faith of Qoheleth," *World and World* 7(1987):253–60.

———. "Qoheleth's 'Quarrel' with the Fathers." In *From Faith to Faith: Essays in Honor of Donald G. Miller on his Seventieth Birthday,* edited by Dikran Y. Hadidian, 235–45. Pittsburgh: Pickwick, 1981.

Ogden, Graham S. *Qoheleth.* Sheffield: Journal for the Study of the Old Testament, 1987.

Literature Cited

Adams, A. K., ed. *The Home Book of Humorous Quotations.* New York: Dodd, Mead, 1969.

Augustine. *On Christian Doctrine,* translated by D. W. Robertson Jr. New York: Macmillan, 1958.

Beaudoin, Tom R. *Virtual Faith: The Irreverent Spiritual Quest of Generation X.* San Francisco: Jossey-Bass, 1998.

Bethge, Eberhard. *Dietrich Bonhoeffer: Theologian, Christian, Contemporary.* London: Collins, 1970.

Bolyki, János. *Jesu Tischgemeinschaften.* Wissenschaftliche Untersuchungen zum Neuen Testament 96. Tübingen: J. C. B. Mohr (Paul Siebeck), 1998.

Bonhoeffer, Dietrich. *Letters and Papers from Prison.* 2d ed., edited by E. Bethge. New York: Macmillan, 1971.

Brink, André. *The Novel: Language and Narrative from Cervantes to Calvino.* New York: New York University Press, 1998.

Brown, William P. *The Ethos of the Cosmos: The Genesis of Moral Imagination in the Bible.* Grand Rapids: Wm. B. Eerdmans, 1999.

———. *Character in Crisis: A Fresh Approach to the Wisdom Literature of the Old Testament.* Grand Rapids: Wm. B. Eerdmans, 1996.

Buck, Pearl S. *My Several Worlds: A Personal Record.* New York: John Day, 1954.

Burkes, Shannon. *Death in Qoheleth and Egyptian Biographies of the Late Period.* Society of Biblical Literature Dissertation Series, vol. 170. Atlanta: Society of Biblical Literature, 1999.

Campbell, Charles. "Principalities, Powers, and Preaching." *Interpretation* 51(1997):384–401.

Camus, Albert. *The Myth of Sisyphus and Other Essays,* translated by J. O'Brien. New York: Alfred A. Knopf, 1955.

Christianson, Eric S. *A Time to Tell: Narrative Strategies in Ecclesiastes.* Journal for the Study of the Old Testament Supplement Series 280. Sheffield: Sheffield Academic Press, 1998.

Crenshaw, James L. *Ecclesiastes.* Old Testament Library. Philadelphia: Westminster, 1987.

Crüsemann, Frank. "The Unchangeable World: The 'Crisis of Wisdom' in Koheleth." In *The God of the Lowly: Socio-Historical Interpretations of the Bible* edited by W. Schottroff and W. Stegemann, translated by M. J. O'Connell, 57–77. Maryknoll: Orbis, 1984.

Dalley, Stephanie. *Myths from Mesopotamia: Creation, The Flood, Gilgamesh, and Others.* World's Classic. Oxford: Oxford University Press, 1991.

Dittes, James. *Men at Work: Life Beyond the Office.* Louisville: Westminster John Knox, 1996.

Fontaine, Carole R. *Traditional Sayings in the Old Testament.* Bible and Literature Series 5. Sheffield: Almond, 1982.

Fox, Michael V. "Aging and Death in Qohelet 12." *Journal for the Study of the Old Testament* 42(1988):59–71.

———. "The Meaning of *Hebel* for Qohelet." *Journal of Biblical Literature* 105(1986):409–27.

———. "Frame-Narrative and Composition in the Book of Qohelet." *Hebrew Union College Annual* 48(1977):83–106.

Gordis, Robert. *Koheleth: The Man and His World.* 3d ed. New York: Schocken, 1968.

Gorssen, Leo. "La cohérence de la conception de Dieu dans l'Ecclésiaste." *Ephemerides theologicae lovanienses* 46(1970):282–324.

Gunn, Janet V. "Autobiography." In *The Encyclopedia of Religion,* vol. 2, edited by M. Eliade, 7–11. New York: Macmillan, 1987.

Gussow, Mel. "For Saul Bellow, Seeing the Earth with Fresh Eyes." *New York Times,* May 26, 1997.

Havel, Vaclav. *Disturbing the Peace.* New York: Vintage, 1991.

Hertzberg, H. W. *Der Prediger.* Kommentar zum Alten Testament 17/4–5. Gütersloh: Gerd Mohn, 1963.

Jacobsen, Thorkild. *The Treasures of Darkness: A History of Mesopotamian Religion.* New Haven: Yale University Press, 1976.

Jones, Brian W. "From Gilgamesh to Qoheleth." In *The Bible in the Light of Cuneiform Literature: Scripture in Context III,* edited by W. W. Hallo et al., 349–79. Ancient Near Eastern Texts and Studies 8. Lewiston, N. Y.: Edwin Mellen, 1990.

Kierkegaard, Søren. *Fear and Trembling and The Sickness Unto Death,*

141

translated by W. Lowrie. Princeton: Princeton University Press, 1941.

Kingsolver, Barbara. *Animal Dreams*. New York: HarperCollins, 1991.

Knohl, Israel. "Between Voice and Silence: The Relationship between Prayer and Temple Cult." *Journal of Biblical Literature* 115(1996): 17–30.

Kovacs, Maureen G. *The Epic of Gilgamesh*. Stanford: Stanford University Press, 1989.

Levine, Étan. *The Aramaic Version of Qohelet*. New York: Sepher-Hermon, 1978.

Lichtheim, Miriam. *Ancient Egyptian Literature*, vol. 3. Berkeley: University of California Press, 1980.

Lindenberger, James D. *The Aramaic Proverbs of Ahiqar*. Baltimore: Johns Hopkins University Press, 1983.

Mays, James L. "Justice: Perspectives from the Prophetic Tradition." *Interpretation* 37(1983):5–17. Reprinted in *Prophecy in Israel: Search for an Identity*, edited by D. L. Petersen, 144–58. Philadelphia: Fortress, 1987.

Meilaender, Gilbert. "The Everyday C. S. Lewis." *First Things* 85 (1998):27–33.

Melville, Herman. *Moby Dick, or The Whale*. New York: Random House, 1930.

Murphy, Roland E. *Ecclesiastes*. Word Biblical Commentary 23A. Dallas: Word Books, 1992.

Norris, Kathleen. "Incarnational Language." *Christian Century* 114/22(7/30–8/6/97):699.

Otto, Rudolph. *The Idea of the Holy*. New York: Oxford University Press, 1969.

Pritchard, James B., ed. *Ancient Near Eastern Texts Relating to the Old Testament*. 3d ed. Princeton: Princeton University Press, 1969.

Robinson, Henry Wheeler. *Inspiration and Revelation in the Old Testament*. Oxford: Clarendon, 1946.

Rahner, Karl. *Belief Today*. New York: Sheed and Ward, 1967.

Rudman, Dominic. "A Note on the Dating of Ecclesiastes." *Catholic Biblical Quarterly* 61(1999):47–52.

Scott, Robert B. Y. *Proverbs, Ecclesiastes*. Anchor Bible 18. Garden City: Doubleday, 1965.

Seow, Choon-Leong. "Qoheleth's Eschatological Poem." *Journal of Biblical Literature* 118(1999):209–34.

———. *Ecclesiastes*. Anchor Bible 18C. New York: Doubleday, 1997.

———. "Linguistic Evidence and the Dating of Qoheleth." *Journal of Biblical Literature* 115(1996):643–66.

————. "Qoheleth's Autobiography." In *Fortunate the Eyes that See: Essays in Honor of David Noel Freedman in Celebration of his Seventieth Birthday*, edited by A. B. Beck *et al.* 257–82. Grand Rapids: Wm. B. Eerdmans, 1995.

Tamez, Elsa. "Living Wisely in the Midst of Absurdity: Meditations from the Book of Ecclesiastes." *Church and Society* 86(1996): 28–42.

————. "The Preacher and the New World Order." *The Other Side* 31/5(1995):22–28.

Tigay, J. H. *The Evolution of the Gilgamesh Epic*. Philadelphia: University of Pennsylvania Press, 1982.

Towner, W. Sibley. "Ecclesiastes." In *The New Interepreter's Bible*, vol. 5, 265–360. Nashville: Abingdon, 1997.

Twain, Mark. "Letter to the Earth." In *Letters from the Earth*, edited by B. Devoto, 117–22. New York: Harper & Row, 1942.

Updike, John. "Forward." In Karl Barth. *Wolfgang Amadeus Mozart*, 7–12. Grand Rapids: Wm. B. Eerdmans, 1987.

Van Leeuwen, Raymond C. "Proverbs 30:21–23 and the Biblical World Upside Down." *Journal of Biblical Literature* 105(1986):599–610.